DRAMMA GIOCOSO
FOUR CONTEMPORARY PERSPECTIVES ON THE MOZART/DA PONTE OPERAS

This tenth publication in the series
"Collected Writings of the Orpheus Institute"
is edited by Darla Crispin

DRAMMA GIOCOSO

Four Contemporary Perspectives on the Mozart/Da Ponte operas

Julian Rushton
Stefan Rohringer
Sergio Durante
James Webster

COLLECTED WRITINGS OF THE
ORPHEUS
INSTITUTE

Leuven University Press
2012

CONTENTS

PREFACE

At the end of Mozart and Da Ponte's *Dramma giocoso*, the titular anti-hero, Don Giovanni, confronts his fate and exits the stage in a dramatic plunging into hellfire. In the 'Prelude' to *Joseph and his Brothers*, aptly subtitled 'Descent into Hell', Thomas Mann sets the scene for his re-telling of the familiar Biblical story, in which he contemplates the mysterious, ultimately ungraspable nature of human history. Describing its characteristic of receding from our comprehension just as we sense that we are gaining understanding, Mann articulates a dilemma, which we find today at the heart of much research:

> For the deeper we sound, the further down into the lower world of the past we probe and press, the more do we find that the earliest foundations of humanity, its history and culture, reveal themselves unfathomable. No matter to what hazardous lengths we let out our line they still withdraw again, and further, into the depths. Again and further are the right words, *for the unresearchable plays a kind of mocking game with our researching ardours [my emphasis]*; it offers apparent holds and goals, behind which, when we have gained them, new reaches of the past still open out – as happens to the coastwise voyager, who finds no end to his journey, for behind each headland of clayey dune he conquers, fresh headlands and new distances lure him on'.[1]

Scholars will always be 'lured on' by the 'fresh headlands and new distances' of the Mozart-Da Ponte operas; we, in turn, will continue to have opportunities to travel with these thinkers as they let out their scholarly line to greater – and sometimes doubtless hazardous – lengths in the hope of illuminating new layers of the apparently endless depth of these works.

In the current volume, the work of the four contributors explores what lies 'behind each headland' of three of the strong concerns

1. Thomas Mann, *Joseph and his Brothers*, tr. H.T. Lowe-Porter, (New York: Penguin Books Ltd., 1984), p. 3.

of music scholarship today: the enfranchisement of performers in discussions on music analysis; the search for more holistic approaches to theoretical systems; and the quest for a more richly contextualised space in which to assess the nature of operatic work – including shifts between conception and final realisation of works according to the effects of performing works in specific national contexts.

The collection opens with Julian Rushton's analysis of opera arias. Rushton issues an important reminder that opera is a particularly 'collective' endeavour, and that Mozart's tailoring of operas to specific singers is a cue for us to note more carefully, and through detailed studies, the emergence of characterization as a process of collaboration. With recourse to specific examples from the Mozart-Da Ponte operas, and a deeper examination of aspects of specific arias from *Don Giovanni,* Rushton demonstrates how establishing a strongly-anchored historical basis for the discussion reveals ramifications for today's musical performances in the act of collaborative re-creation. His ideas about collaboration are also echoed in the second and third articles of the collection.

Stefan Rohringer's contribution concerns *Don Giovanni's* Don Ottavio, inviting us, both as analysts and performers, to look again at this problematic character. Using this as a starting point, Rohringer outlines the important role of 'tone' – that of the tenor voice – in generating characterization, and how this was to undergo transformation during the progression of the history of opera. Returning to Don Ottavio, Rohringer anchors his theorizing through a provocative reading of the aria, *Il mio tesoro*, concluding that it functions both in terms of the specific character, and as a symbol of the 18th century tenor's increasing disunity in terms of implied social role and dramatic function.

This aspect of 'situatedness' is given broader scope in Sergio Durante's historical contextualisation of the libretto of *Don Giovanni*, in which he reminds us of the importance of such figures as E.T.A. Hoffmann in transforming the reception of opera in the 19th century. More significantly, Durante explores the ramifications of the impossible quest for a 'universal standard text' – a concept that undoubtedly 'plays a kind of mocking game with our researching ardours'. For Durante, though, the problems of this search become a lens through which we can view and better understand the links between opera and cultural identification, demonstrating once again the need to provide contexts, rather than to read musical works – and in particular operas – in isolation.

Taking up this call, but with a more pronounced emphasis upon music analysis, James Webster argues for a more comprehensive, contextual kind of study – one that releases works from strictly monadic readings and places them more vividly within both their own contemporary social and historical contexts and those in which they are eventually read. In common with Rushton, Webster cautions against analytical approaches generated by the desire to understand 'absolute music', and their concomitant models of 'unity'. His own analysis, focussing upon Act IV of *Le Nozze di Figaro*, posits acceptance of open (unresolved) rather than 'closed' readings.

The collective endeavours of the authors of this volume, contemplating, as most of them have done, Don Giovanni's own 'descent into Hell', confirm the Mozart-Da Ponte operas as 'becoming' the same human history that they prompt their listeners to contemplate. Their complex, ultimately unfathomable, nature invites us into difficult but instructive reflections on that history, and into speculations about our own present day and our own states of being. If Don Giovanni's 'fall' comes about, in part, because of his inability to change, then we are aptly invited to think differently through contemplation of this and other works that allow us, from our own historical standpoints, to project forwards as to how we might approach opera in the future. As Thomas Mann implies, the fact that definitive truths endlessly withdraw 'again and further into the depths' need not be, for us, and our research ardours, a descent into Hell but, instead, an alluring prospect richly stocked with fresh headlands and new distances.

Darla M. Crispin

'BY THEIR ARIAS SHALL YE KNOW THEM': CHARACTERIZATION IN ARIA-BASED OPERA

Julian Rushton

When a student, and thus easily influenced, I read the first edition of Joseph Kerman's *Opera as Drama*.[1] 45 years on, I still broadly agree with his dictum that in opera 'the imaginative articulation for the drama is provided by music'.[2] But the music of an opera does not come into being in creative isolation, and in Mozart's time composers had to accommodate the views of patrons; the theatre management; the poet; and, not least, the singers. From the start of Mozart's operatic career, he liked to fit arias to singers as a tailor fits a suit of clothes.[3] One aim in showing such concern for singers was to get them on his side. That was because the effectiveness of the performance depended on their commitment; and that in turn might produce another commission. Thus I can hardly suppose that Mozart's concern for singers was unusual. Possibly he accommodated them better than other composers; but then he did most things better than other composers.

An operatic character was thus a collaborative creation. To put it simply (perhaps too simply), both the poet (who usually acted as stage director) and the composer collaborated with the singer for whom the role was intended. This practice may never have been universal, but it continued into the nineteenth century. Since then, changing theatrical practices, not least the concentration of the repertory on older works, has reduced the amount of direct collaboration with singers, but their involvement can still be a factor in newly composed operas, for instance those of Benjamin Britten. In Mozart's time it was routine to compose with a particular singer in mind. The composer carefully studied

1. Joseph Kerman, *Opera as Drama*, New York 1956.
2. Kerman, *Opera as Drama*, new revised edition, London 1989, pp. 1 and 7.
3. Leopold Mozart's letter of 24 November 1770.

the range, tessitura, agility, power, and dramatic flair of the singers intended for the opera's first production.[4] With Mozart at least there are well documented instances of singers' influence on his work in *Idomeneo* and *Die Entführung aus dem Serail*, and there is no reason to regard these as atypical; we know of them rather than others merely because, when working on these operas, he was writing regularly to his father.[5] In Vienna in the 1780s, other operas had greater success than Mozart's, and that could hardly have come about unless (for instance) Salieri and Martín y Soler also studied the singers assiduously. They were in most cases the same as those who sang Mozart's works.

Nevertheless, operas also succeeded when revived or performed in another city, with a new cast. New productions and revivals involved various kinds of compromise. In such cases, what becomes of the notion of the singer as collaborator? Paisiello's *Il barbiere di Siviglia*, premiered in St Petersburg in 1782, was a great success in Vienna when performed by the local opera buffa troupe. The cast included singers who later took part in its sequel, *Le nozze di Figaro*. *Figaro*'s triumph in Prague led in turn to the commission for *Don Giovanni*. Thus when composing *Don Giovanni* for Prague in 1787, Mozart knew nearly all of the singers from their roles in *Figaro*.[6] Nevertheless, it is virtually certain that he also bore in mind the need to accommodate the singers in Vienna, where *Don Giovanni* was produced in May 1788.

Thus when composing *Don Giovanni* he probably had in mind the original cast of *Figaro*. But by May 1788, several members of the *Figaro* cast were no longer in Vienna. Nancy Storace and Michael Kelly returned to England early in 1787, so Mozart knew they would not be available for *Don Giovanni*. The original Count

---

4. Mozart did have difficulties with some singers when as a boy he composed *Mitridate* for Milan (1770), and *Lucio Silla* (1772) when the title role was recast for an inexperienced singer at the last moment. His problems with the castrato Dal Prato in *Idomeneo* (1781) are documented in his letters. See Julian Rushton (ed.), *The New Grove Guide to Mozart's Operas*, New York 2006.
5. See the essays by Stanley Sadie and Mark Everist in Julian Rushton (ed.), *W. A. Mozart: Idomeneo*, Cambridge 1993, and Thomas Bauman, *W. A. Mozart: Die Entführung aus dem Serail*, Cambridge 1987.
6. The main exception was Baglioni, the Don Ottavio.

Almaviva, Stefano Mandini, left for Naples in January 1788, after creating a role in Salieri's *Axur, re d'Ormus.*[7] So in 1787, when composing *Don Giovanni,* Mozart probably expected Mandini to play the title-role in the Vienna production. Moreover in Vienna, as Stefan Rohringer has reminded us, there was a tenor problem.[8] Mozart might have expected Vincenzo Calvesi to be available for Don Ottavio, but he too left for Naples early in 1788, returning to Vienna in time to create Ferrando in *Così fan tutte.* Mozart wrote a new aria for tenor, 'Dalla sua pace', perhaps to make way for the extra scene for Catarina Cavalieri ('In quali eccessi ... Mi tradì'), although it is usually assumed that the new tenor, Morella, was unequal to the demands of 'Il mio tesoro'.[9] The inclusion of both arias, however, merely strengthens our impression of Ottavio's essential weakness.

I would argue that in later productions, even those without the benefit of the presence and participation of the composer and poet, singers are still collaborators, albeit now in an act of re-creation. However minor the changes in musical performance, and however well the singers adapt to material designed for others, they will always affect the perception of character. Sometimes, if the composer was absent, singers suited themselves by using someone else's music, a fate that befell several of Mozart's works after his death; but this is a part of reception history beyond the scope of the present discussion. Most singers taking over

7. After the first performances in January and February 1788, there was a gap before *Axur* was presented again, in April, when another singer must have taken over Mandini's role. Data on performances from Dorothea Link, *The National Court Theatre in Mozart's Vienna,* Oxford 1998, 23–190.

8. Stefan Rohringer, 'The two Don Ottavios: Mozart's modified perspective on his primo uomo in the Vienna version of Don Giovanni', paper delivered at the International Orpheus Academy for Music & Theory, 26 March 2008, and published in this volume in revised form as 'Don Ottavio and the History of the Tenor Voice'.

9. Dexter Edge deploys persuasive evidence from the Vienna orchestral parts, which contain both tenor arias, to suggest that the decision to cut 'Il mio tesoro' need not have been a consequence of adding 'Dalla sua pace', in 'The Orchestral Parts from the First Viennese Production of *Don Giovanni* in 1788', paper read at the Annual Meeting of the American Musicological Society, Toronto, 3 November 2000. A new review of the evidence has been undertaken by Ian Woodfield, *The Vienna* Don Giovanni, Woodbridge, The Boydell Press, 2010.

roles composed for someone else would adapt their performing techniques as necessary. Where Vienna is concerned, some caution is needed, as we do not always know who sang which role; the Burgtheater operated a repertory system, and roles were often shared.[10] In Paisiello's *Barbiere* both Nancy Storace and Luisa Laschi sang Rosina (the only female role) in different performances. No wonder, when Mozart composed the sequel, there was some uncertainty about which of them would sing the Countess and which Susanna. Mozart was involved in early revivals of both *Figaro* and *Don Giovanni*. *Figaro* was taken over intact for Prague, but when *Don Giovanni* came to Vienna it was enlarged with a comic duet for Zerlina and Leporello, designed for singers who had appeared in *Figaro*, Laschi and Francesco Benucci.[11] Mozart also composed new arias for the Vienna *Don Giovanni* in 1788, for the revived *Figaro* in 1789, all for singers new to the opera buffa troupe. With *Figaro*, it is likely that the original singers were used where possible.[12] However, the new, and highly paid, prima donna, Adriana Ferrarese, possessed different talents from those of Storace. For her Mozart composed 'Un moto di gioia', although he doubted whether she could sing simply enough, and 'Al desio di chi t'adora', which probably suited her well.[13] 'Al desio' is a rondò; and, like Anna's 'Non mi dir', it is the last aria before the finale, the exalted position proper to a prima donna's rondò. *Figaro* was performed more often with Ferrarese than with Storace, so 'Al desio' was heard more often in Vienna in Mozart's lifetime than the music it replaced, 'Deh vieni non tardar', which is virtually always preferred today.

---

10. Link, *The National Court Theatre*, pp. 487–8.
11. Benucci was the first Figaro; Laschi (also known by her married name, Mombelli), was the first Countess in *Figaro*.
12. Besides Benucci, the original Bartolo and Cherubino were available (Francesco and Dorotea Bussani). All three were in the original cast for *Così fan tutte* (Guglielmo, Alfonso, and Despina).
13. On 'Un moto di gioia', letter of 19 August 1789: on 'Al desio', Zinzendorf's diary for 7 May 1790 praises her singing in the 'letter' duet and the 'rondeau'; see Link, *The National Court Theatre*, p. 355. In emulation, rondò arias were designed for her in Salieri's *La cifra* (December 1789) and in *Così fan tutte* (January 1790). See Mary Hunter's review of John A. Rice, *Antonio Salieri and Viennese Opera*, *Journal of the Royal Musical Association*, 125/1 (2000), p. 125.

Presumably other singers were better than Ferrarese at adapting themselves to existing roles. By now Laschi too had left Vienna, so Caterina Cavalieri (the first Konstanze) sang the Countess. Minor changes to her shorter rondò ('Dove sono') may have been made to accommodate her.[14] Thus in 1789, other than the role of Susanna, *Figaro* was not radically changed, even with new singers involved. This, however, does not mean that the 1786 cast was less important in shaping the roles in the first place; and it also means that the characterizations, especially of Susanna, are likely to have seemed a little different in 1789.

* * *

Operas arise as a union of words, music, spectacle, and the minds and bodies of the original singers. For us, the original spectacle is mainly lost; and the original singers are dead. But we can try to reconstruct singers' capabilities by studying what they performed, with particular attention to arias actually written for them.[15] Arias are more significant than ensembles, because, as Mozart insisted at the time of *Idomeneo*, ensembles are the domain of the composer.[16] But arias tell us what a particular singer could do effectively; and the outcome is an operatic persona, a character. The presentation of a rounded personality in opera is inextricably involved with the voice. I have suggested elsewhere that Mozart's understanding of this point is demonstrated even when he deliberately did not exploit all the capabilities of a particular singer well known to him.[17]

---

14. Alan Tyson, *Mozart: Studies of the Autograph Scores*, Cambridge (Mass) 1987, pp. 319–21. The changes make the aria shorter, with a short rather than a sustained a", but with a new florid passage whose difficulty falls far short of what Mozart composed for Cavalieri in *Die Entführung aus dem Serail.*
15. In addition to published scores, see Dorothea Link (ed.), *Arias for Nancy Storace, Mozart's First Susanna*, Middleton, Wisconsin 2002, and *Arias for Francesco Benucci, Mozart's First Figaro* Middleton, Wisconsin 2004.
16. Mozart refused to change the Quartet to accommodate the tenor Raaff; see his letter of 27 December 1780.
17. Julian Rushton, 'Buffo roles in Mozart's Vienna: tessitura and tonality as signs of characterization', in J. Webster and M. Hunter (eds.), *Opera Buffa in Mozart's Vienna*, Cambridge 1997, pp. 406-425 (cited p. 425).

In asserting that the composer contributes so much to characterization, I run up against opposition from the philosopher Peter Kivy, who concludes that Mozart was a 'confidence man'. Kivy has maintained that 'character depth in opera is an "illusion of psychological depth"' or, as he chose to put it later, 'an "aesthetic" or "artistic" effect'. All characterization that is not illusory resides in the libretto.[18] Although Kivy's point is philosophical, and his objective is to praise Mozart, not to diminish his importance, I cannot agree. With Mozart, opera is not a play with inserted songs, or a *comédie mêlée d'ariettes*. In the theatre, we are immediately and strongly affected by the music. The way characters sing tells us more about them than the words, which are frequently inaudible. In assessing a character, we are more likely to be affected by what we see than by the words; and in an aria, what we see may be no more than a singer standing still and delivering the music.

A rounded characterization thus arises from an accumulation of information. Once formed, it may be modified, but not fundamentally changed, in later performances. However, a case against Kivy requires us to show how music makes a difference to interpretation of a character. Don Giovanni's aria 'Metà di voi qua vadano' is sometimes neglected in discussions of his character, because he sings it pretending to be Leporello. Nevertheless, it contains clear 'musical' signs of a defining element in his character: his narcissism. According to psychological theory, narcissism is a characteristic of the compulsive seducer, and we may connect it to what Kierkegaard, and others since, have recognized as an essential blankness in Giovanni.[19] Undoubtedly narcissism is detectable in Giovanni by other means, and an interesting

18. Peter Kivy, 'How did Mozart do it?: Living Conditions in the World of Opera', in *The Fine Art of Repetition*, Cambridge 1993, cited here from pp. 167 (where Kivy cites his earlier *Osmin's Rage. Philosophical Reflections on Opera, Drama and Text*, Princeton 1988) and responses to it, 171, 177.

19. On Kierkegaard see Bernard Williams, 'Don Giovanni as an Idea', in Rushton, *W. A. Mozart: Don Giovanni*, pp. 81–91, reprinted in Williams, *On Opera*, New Haven 2006, pp. 31–42. Kerman, *Opera as Drama* (1989 edition), p. 102; Kerman, 'Reading *Don Giovanni*', in Jonathan Miller (ed.), *The Don Giovanni Book*, London 1990, pp. 108–125.

recent interpretation also neglects 'Metà di voi qua vadano'.[20] In this aria, admittedly, the words 'could' imply narcissism at the point where Giovanni, pretending to be Leporello and addressing Masetto, describes his own accoutrements so that he (or rather Leporello) can be identified. But these words might have been set to quite different music. It is only the music that makes clear that Giovanni 'likes' what he is describing (himself), and it does this by exploiting tessitura and tonality. Pretending to be Leporello, Giovanni darkens his voice so that, in a dim light, and to a dim brain – Masetto's – he can pass for Leporello. The tessitura is accordingly low. But when he describes his beautiful hat and phallic sword, he rises above the bass tessitura habitual for Leporello, into his own baritone domain. The aria is in F, but Giovanni sings rising G major arpeggios to his favourite high d'; and the arpeggios are preceded by F sharps. Such emphatic tonicization of the dominant of the dominant is uncommon in arias, certainly in this opera.[21] No doubt Da Ponte as well as Mozart meant us to understand that Giovanni is immensely pleased with himself, nearly all the time. Da Ponte supplied appropriate words to end of the trio 'Ah taci ingiusto core': 'Più fertile talento del mio, nò, non si dà'. Here, however, self-congratulation is not prominent in the music, or in what we see: our eyes are fixed on Leporello, trying to restrain his laughter, and Elvira, who bears the melodic line, regretting her weakness. Giovanni's words are easily overlooked. It is in arias that Mozart makes characterization most secure.

* * *

Giovanni's narcissism, in words and music, is psychological realism. But this should give us pause. For what has realism to do

---

20. Richard Rusbridger, 'The Internal World of *Don Giovanni*', *International Journal of Psychoanalysis* 89 (2008), pp. 181–194. I am grateful to Dr Rusbridger for an offprint of his article.

21. The arpeggios resemble Leporello's later aria, but also the end of 'Catalogue aria' when Leporello evokes Giovanni's actions. But the point is not the arpeggio itself, but the tessitura and tonal gesture. This discussion emerges from Julian Rushton, 'Buffo roles in Mozart's Vienna', pp. 421–2. On the privileging of d' in Giovanni's role see Andrew Steptoe, *The Mozart-Da Ponte Operas*, Oxford 1988, pp. 203–4.

with opera? If that question seems too sweeping, we may ask instead what realism has to do with eighteenth-century opera; and we may conclude that the right answer is very little – and not only because operatic characters sing all the time, at least in Italian opera. In considering the inhabitants of the world of opera as if they were real people, we cannot ignore this peculiarity. We may treat it merely as a convention, making an obvious comparison with verse drama; real people do not normally speak in Alexandrines, or unrhymed iambic pentameters. But is the verse in verse drama merely a convention? The practice of Shakespeare suggests otherwise: even his tragedies also contain prose, and songs. Operas embrace a range of modes of musical discourse. In recitative, the musical interest is much reduced; the poetic verses are treated like prose, and the notated rhythms are (or may be) treated with considerable freedom in performance. In aria, the music takes over, becoming metrical, and stronger in expression. Aria is thus analogous to poetry rather than prose. But the general effect of poetry in tragedies as diverse as those of Shakespeare, Racine, Schiller, or Eliot, is to make the characters unreal because they appear to us larger than real life. The music of an aria may have a similar effect.

Opera buffa arias can be ranged along a spectrum. At one end, a few arias are delivered, nearly, at the pace of realistic drama; at the other end, many arias stop the action in its tracks. The latter are likely to make greatest demands on the singers' vocal resources, and so make the most potent contribution of singers to characterization. *Le nozze di Figaro* is based on a realistic play, set in modern times, and in prose. But the opera libretto is in verse, which was then subjected to the formal requirements of music. After these manipulations of Beaumarchais' original, the Countess for one, even at the moment of truth and reconciliation in the Act IV finale, becomes a markedly different personality from the woman in the play.

Other than in recitative, the requirements of eighteenth-century music detract from any lingering realism. Even ensembles do not simply (as Kerman's chapter title implies) weld action and music into one continuity.[22] Even in Mozart's liveliest ensembles the action is at a standstill most of the time, while the characters explore their reactions at what, in spoken drama, would be absurd length; an ensemble may even turn into simultaneous soliloquies. In opera this is not absurd because we allow music its right to formal completeness, indeed coherence, on a musical level, and so we suspend any expectation of realism.

Exploring their own emotions is what characters routinely do in arias. There are exceptions. Susanna's 'Venite inginocchiatevi' is intimately wedded to the action.[23] So is 'Metà di voi quà vadano', and Giovanni's serenade is an act; thus the only aria in which he might reveal himself is 'Fin ch'han dal vino'. Kerman has isolated in this an 'anger', at odds with the words, and with the usual connotations of the fast tempo, and the topic, a brilliant contredanse.[24] Giovanni has just suffered some unusual reverses: his failure with Anna, his encounters with Elvira. He puts all this behind him in 'Fin ch'han dal vino' because his infantile compulsions (including narcissism) make him unable to stand criticism.[25] But in another important sense Giovanni is the 'least' narcissistic of operatic characters, because he is untypical of operatic persons in general. It is not only the opening scene that is, in Joseph Kerman's words, a 'generic violation'.[26] So is the entire personality, or blankness, of the title-role. Even in 'Fin ch'han dal vino' he does not address his feelings directly to the audience. For it is also a plan of campaign for the afternoon party, and an act put on for the benefit of Leporello. Thus 'Fin ch'han dal vino' hides as much as it reveals.

---

22. Kerman, *Opera as Drama*, chapter 4, 'Action and the Musical Continuity'. Although chapter 5 is 'Mozart', chapter 4 discusses the trios from *Figaro* and *Don Giovanni*.
23. James Webster, 'The Analysis of Mozart's Arias', in Cliff Eisen (ed.), *Mozart Studies*, Oxford 1991, pp. 101–199; on 'Venite inginocchiatevi', pp. 183–7.
24. Kerman, 'Reading *Don Giovanni*', pp. 117–120.
25. Rusbridger refers to 'phallic narcissism', 'The Internal World of *Don Giovanni*', p. 187. I suggest it was not only phallic. At least Giovanni *knows* he cannot stand criticism: 'Non soffro opposizione' (Act II, scene 1).
26. Kerman, 'Reading *Don Giovanni*', p. 114.

In a searching essay on *Don Giovanni*, Kerman echoes Edward T. Cone's 'startling' – Cone's word – if ultimately unsustainable notion of operatic characters as composers.[27] Kerman refers to the 'characters' – not the composer's – manipulation of musical material; and he finds that in this respect, Giovanni is less musically inventive than the other characters.[28] Musical invention in soliloquy is aimed inward, to the character singing, and outward, to the audience. The rhetorical strands become more complicated if there are people on stage who are known to be listening, as Ottavio listens to Anna's 'Non mi dir', and still more complex if the character is unaware of being overheard.[29] Unless drama is to be impoverished by banishing soliloquy, we must accept that a character who, realistically, is merely thinking something over, nevertheless speaks (sings) these thoughts out loud.

Dramatic characters often seem aware of the existence of the audience; indeed, not to be aware of the audience requires a rigorous realism perhaps only obtainable in film. Addressing the audience is common in opera, as in spoken drama, although overt instances are usually confined to comic roles, like Leporello. 'Notte giorno faticar' is otherwise addressed to thin air, like Sganarelle's concluding lines in Molière's *Dom Juan*: 'Ah! mes gages! mes gages! Voilà, par sa mort, un chacun satisfait ... il n'y a que moi seul de malheureux! Mes gages! mes gages! mes gages!' Whereas at the end of Mozart's *Don Giovanni* everyone steps out of character, losing individuality in the fugato, Molière's Sganarelle steps out of character to point the moral, while remaining in character to worry about his pay.

Despite its ostensible realism of setting, *Le nozze di Figaro* includes several soliloquies. Only one of these is overheard: this is Susanna's soliloquy in the garden, including 'Deh vieni non tardar' (or 'Al desio'). Susanna, of course, *intends* Figaro to

---

27. Edward T. Cone, 'The World of Opera and its Inhabitants', in *Music: a View from Delft*, Chicago 1989, p. 130.

28. Kerman, 'Reading *Don Giovanni*', pp. 120–1.

29. The rhetorical lines of communication are more convoluted still if we enter the composer and the original singer into the equation. See Julian Rushton, 'Mozart's art of rhetoric: understanding an opera seria aria', in *Contemporary Music Review*, vol. 17 part 3 (1998), pp. 15-29.

overhear her singing. There is no exact equivalent in the play; but in witnessing the opera, neither the audience nor Figaro regard Susanna as insane, even though she 'speaks' (sings) out loud. The Prague version of *Don Giovanni* is unusual because, after 'Notte giorno faticar', the only soliloquies are those of Elvira.[30] Both are overheard by Giovanni and Leporello. So it is not a sign of mental instability when Elvira sings aloud of her betrayal in the aria 'Ah, chi mi dice mai quel barbaro dov'è', or in the trio 'Ahi taci ingiusto core', although in both cases she herself must believe that she is addressing an empty street and, indeed, even in the latter case, singing an aria. Molière, who provides the model for Elvira, reverses the situation: she enters and at once accosts Don Juan.[31] This resembles her later entrances in Act I of the opera, when she surprises him seducing Zerlina ('Fermati, scellerato') and addressing unctuous remarks to Anna ('Ah ti ritrovo ancor, perfido mostro'). These entries are in recitative, but her entrance aria – 'Ah, chi mi dice mai' – is overheard, and converted into a trio by the *pertichini* of Giovanni and Leporello, an effect repeated when 'Ah, taci ingiusto core' becomes a trio.

Elvira is impulsive, but she is not insane. In the quartet, Giovanni fails to persuade Anna and Ottavio that she is mad, and the others recognize in her a lady of gentle breeding in distress. They are surely the more reliable witnesses. So Elvira utters intimate thoughts out loud; and we, the opera audience, must accept this behaviour, or fail to understand a quintessentially operatic experience.

* * *

Operatic characters 'have' to act unrealistically, because the tempo of their activities is regulated by the demands of the music. But we cannot simply overlook this lack of realism, or deny that it affects our understanding of these characters as people. They are a special human type; one that clamours for attention. Rather than considering them, with Cone, as a special kind of composer,

30. The Vienna version modifies this by the addition of two soliloquies that are not overheard, Ottavio's 'Dalla sua pace' and Elvira's scena 'In quali eccessi – Mi tradì quell'alma ingrata'.

31. Molière, *Dom Juan*, Act I scene 3.

I suggest the distinguishing feature of operatic characters is that they are nearly all egotistical, even narcissistic; but this egotism, this narcissism, is 'normal' in opera. I do not, of course, mean leading singers in their professional capacity, although they are proverbially vain. I mean the fictional characters in the drama. Even Leporello, in 'Notte, giorno faticar', draws us, the audience, into his self-centred complaint. 'Voglio far il gentiluomo' crudely recalls Figaro's class resentment, expressed in 'Se vuol ballare' (and more explicitly in Beaumarchais). Like the Count in *Figaro*, Giovanni can make free with women because he had the good luck to be born rich. I believe that in forming the role of Leporello, Mozart had in mind not only Felice Ponziani, who created the role in Prague, but also Benucci, the first Figaro. Both roles suggest that Benucci was rather good both at expressing resentment, and at appearing pleased with himself (an essential part of Figaro's personality, leading to the misguided plotting that rebounds on him in the central finale; we may also hear self-satisfaction in another Benucci role, Guglielmo). We can hear this justifiable resentment, and some less justifiable self-satisfaction, in Leporello's personality as well. Self-centredness merges into narcissism when an operatic character feels impelled to dominate the stage, to confide to the audience or to other characters feelings of love, anger, indignation, or fear, or to express satisfaction at his, or her, own cleverness, or in one special case the accomplishments of someone else. In the catalogue aria, Leporello takes pride in displaying his master's achievements – precisely those that, in 'Notte giorno faticar', he envies. Revealing the catalogue allows Leporello, in his own way, to humiliate Elvira. So he blossoms with a vicarious satisfaction: he may not be much of a seducer himself, but he serves the greatest seducer of all.

Many of the feelings so strongly projected in operatic arias are the type of emotion that in real life would tend to make one cautious, silent; perhaps sulky, withdrawn. Representation of such feelings could work well in spoken theatre, but they are not conducive to musical setting. In opera such feelings must be openly displayed, to us and often to other characters. Hence operatic characters are exceptionally prone to self-dramatization. Even if the libretto makes someone appear meek, obedient, or conformist, that character may still dominate the stage, and display a demanding personality. Even a good girl – *una buona figluola* – may, at certain points, demand that we pay attention to the depth and complexity of her feelings. An obvious example is Michaela in *Carmen*, in her Act III aria. But the type exists in the eighteenth century. Ilia in *Idomeneo* is gentle and self-sacrificing, but also tough; her steely resolve, well contrasted to the hysterical Elettra, emerges in her two soliloquies. Nothing and no-one – not even Idamante whom she loves – matters as much as her inner conflict between love and duty. She expresses her love fully and directly only in her third aria, 'Zefiretti lusinghieri', but her conscience is clear because she believes the object of temptation, Idamante, is far away. It is only with her final entrance that Ilia offers herself for sacrifice, and by ceasing to be all ego, she brings about the *lieto fine* – in recitative.

We rightly sympathize with Pamina, singing 'Ach, ich fühl's'. James Webster has convincingly shown that in this aria, and in others, the action does not in fact stand still. In this case, the orchestral coda 'cries out her grief' as Pamina leaves the stage 'more articulately than she can herself'.[32] In Mozart, Webster reminds us, aria is drama. Pamina's feelings are poured out before us, and before Tamino and Papageno; but it is typical of dramatic arias that she thinks mainly of herself: '... ewig hin der Liebe Glück! Nimmer kommt ihr Wonnestunden meinem Herzen mehr zurück!' If these words were spoken, we might wonder why she does not realise that Tamino, who, as she well knows, is undergoing trials, may also be having difficulties; if an actor wanted our sympathy in such a position (and what actor does not?), she would look into his eyes and see his suffering. Pamina is of course being put through a trial of her own, which leads her to contemplate suicide. By such trials, Ilia and Pamina come to a higher level of understanding, as do other characters in these operas, including Papageno. But on the way to that understanding, even they appear as much self-centred as altruistic.

32. Webster, 'The Analysis of Mozart's Arias', p. 196.

Sincere altruistic sentiments are not unknown even in arias, for instance in Don Ottavio's 'Dalla sua pace', the soliloquy added to the Vienna *Don Giovanni*, probably because the new tenor was not fully equal to 'Il mio tesoro'. But Ottavio is not a character widely admired, because of his abject dependence on his beloved Anna. In the previous scene, Anna's 'Or sai chi l'onore' reaches extraordinary heights of emotional intensity. Her moral rectitude is matched by the aria's stubborn ternary form, even the first section ending in the tonic key, like a miniature version of a Baroque Da Capo aria. The only breach in the solidity of this utterance comes in the reprise: the interrupted cadence, which could simply have prolonged, and emphasized, closure, seems to breach her confidence, as she gasps out words inexactly remembered from the middle section: 'Rammenta ... la piaga ... rimira ...il sangue ...'. But she quickly regains control to end 'Vendetta ti chiedo, la chiedo il tuo cor'. If this is obsession, it seems morally justifiable, but it is hardly altruistic: that her intense desire for vengeance may bring difficulty and danger for Ottavio hardly occurs to her. Anna is an avenging fury, like Elettra; both are driven by egoism to a point where their own interests are all that matters. Thus arias like 'Or sai chi l'onore' that are heard by another character are often just as much vehicles for a character's self-absorption as soliloquies. Ottavio is again an exception, but although 'Il mio tesoro', as the libretto makes clear, is addressed to three other characters, it could easily be a soliloquy, for they do not react at all. Altruism makes Ottavio, in operatic terms, an underdeveloped character, perhaps a little boring, even a wimp, despite the later history of 'Il mio tesoro' as a tenor showpiece. Eventually he fetches *ministri di giustizia*, who (in the libretto) enter at the end. This dependence on official forces of law and order makes him a pale reflection of the noble Ottavio at the court of the King of Castille, in Tirso da Molina's drama.[33]

33. Ottavio's weak ego is well, if tediously, reflected in Joseph Losey's film, where both his arias seem to have caused the director serious embarrassment. His recourse to the police and its neglect in modern production is discussed in Lior Barshack, 'The Sovereignty of Pleasure. Sexual and Political Freedom in the Operas of Mozart and Da Ponte', in *Law & Literature*, vol. 20 no.1 (2008), pp. 47–67.

As critics have noted, the sisters in *Così fan tutte* engage energetically in self-dramatization in their Act I arias, 'Smanie implacabili' and 'Come scoglio'. In Act II Dorabella's ego is revealed as weaker, and her personality more yielding. Her Act II aria is 'Amore e un ladroncello': love is a thief. This is, intentionally, a cliché, and rhetorical emphasis in the music is correspondingly replaced by self-satisfied charm. Fiordiligi remains fully operatic, as befits the prima donna: Ferrarese brooked no equal.[34] If *Così* were an ordinary opera, her rondò, 'Per pietà', would be the last item before the finale, like 'Al desio' in the 1789 *Figaro*. In that position, Fiordiligi begins what she must believe is her third aria, 'Fra gli amplessi'. She dramatizes her feelings out loud to the audience – and to what she believes is an empty room. But in her self-absorption, she does not notice that Ferrando is listening; 'Fra gli amplessi' becomes a duet. If we find that impossible, or assume Fiordiligi is insane, rather than overwrought, we again miss an essential aspect of operatic characterization.

* * *

Le nozze di Figaro stands somewhat outside the rules of normal opera. There are many reasons for this, beyond its dramatic origins and Mozart's unusual deployment of sonata-like forms. In *Figaro* there is a relatively low incidence of self-dramatization, and not merely because there are so many ensembles. This observation bears on the role of the singers in creating the opera. The Countess has two soliloquies, addressed to us and to an empty room; significantly, neither has a direct source in Beaumarchais. If the Countess – a much loved character – appears less egotistical than Anna, Elvira, or Fiordiligi, it is partly because her arias – the cavatina ('Porgi amor') and the concise rondò ('Dove sono') – are relatively short.[35] But the Countess is not the force within

34. Assuming that her monthly payment in the year ending February 1789 was maintained, she would have received 5400 florins per annum, 20% more than Storace or Laschi. The account books are missing for the next three years, so there is no entry for Luisa Villeneuve, who sang Dorabella. See the account books transcribed in Link, *The National Court Theatre*, pp. 399–478.
35. On these arias see Webster, 'The Analysis of Mozart's Arias', pp. 151–174.

the action that Susanna is. Susanna is a miracle: an operatic character who appears almost realistic, despite her practice of singing duets. These include the first two numbers, so her influence is established at once, and is felt throughout the opera. Susanna's personality was modified in 1789, when, in the guise of Ferrarese, she sings a rondò, 'Al desio'. This is no longer the Susanna of Nancy Storace, who sang 'Deh vieni non tardar'. The originally conceived rondò, and the 1789 version, 'Al desio', too obviously suggest the Countess herself, rather than the maidservant.[36]

But why did Mozart not write a rondò for Storace/Susanna? The original plan of Act IV of *Figaro* did include one, 'Non tardar, amato bene', of which the opening is sketched in the key of E flat.[37] But it was abandoned in favour of the F major serenade-like 'Deh vieni, non tardar'. Storace was a versatile actress. Although her voice was perhaps less strong than that of her rival Laschi, she had an outstanding stage presence. This is confirmed by reports of her acting and dancing in *La grotta di Trofonio*.[38] A few months after *Figaro*, late in 1786, Storace played Sofronia in *Gli equivoci*, which has a libretto by Da Ponte. As prima donna, she has the last aria before the finale in which the comedy of errors is disentangled. But 'Potessi di piangere' is not a rondò: it is a ternary form, in C major, based (for no obvious reason) on a Scottish folk-song.[39] It seems that Storace could express pathos effectively through relatively simple music. *Oscuro* is added to *chiaro* in a minor-mode middle section, with storm and stress – rapid scales and sudden dynamic changes – making a form that anticipates 'Or sai chi l'onore', though with a more literal reprise. Singing 'Ah s'altro il mio vivere / che pianto non è, / la vita toglie-

36. It should be noted that although she is disguised as the Countess, Figaro has not seen her, and he does not think she *is* the Countess. He knows who is singing. 'Deh vieni' is not an aristocratic piece; 'Al desio' is, although the dramatic situation is precisely the same, and this in itself justifies restoring Mozart's original aria, 'Deh vieni'.
37. Mozart, *Le nozze di Figaro*, ed. Ludwig Finscher, Neue Mozart Ausgabe Serie II, Werkgruppe 5, Band 16 (Kassel: Bärenreiter, 1973), pp. 640–1.
38. See Link, *Arias for Nancy Storace*, p. xi.
39. Link reproduces this aria in *Arias for Nancy Storace*, pp. 82–7. See also Stephen Storace, *Gli equivoci* (ed. Richard Platt), *Musica Britannica* vol. LXXXVI, London 2007.

temi / ch'è morte per me', Storace/Sofronia descends to bottom A flat. The aria has a narrower range, and slightly lower tessitura, than 'Deh vieni, non tardar'. The text is more conventional, and the musical form is markedly less original. At the end, Sofronia is exactly where she started: a suffering wife, waiting for something to happen. James Webster observes of 'Deh vieni non tardar' that it transforms 'Susanna's yearning into outright desire'.[40] The rondò would seem ideal for such dramatic development, because of its two tempi: slow, then allegro, then perhaps *più allegro*. The miracle of 'Deh vieni' is that Mozart achieves this erotic warming in one tempo, while preserving Susanna's essential character.

I infer that Storace, taking seriously her role as a collaborator in characterization, permitted the substitution on dramatic grounds. Perhaps she even welcomed it.[41] For Storace was perfectly capable of singing a difficult rondò. Mozart compensated her with the scena and rondò with piano obbligato, 'Ch'io mi scordi di te', which is in E flat like the abandoned rondò in *Figaro*.[42] This was performed shortly before her departure from Vienna.[43] Already, in Act I of *Gli equivoci*, Storace had sung an elaborate rondò in E flat, 'Ah come in un istante'. This has a range of over two octaves, is longer that any rondò in Mozart's Da Ponte operas, and ends with a demonstration of agility that might have appealed to Ferrarese

40. Webster, 'The Analysis of Mozart's Arias', pp. 181–3, also discussing the rejected rondò 'Non tardar, amato bene'.

41. There is the possibility that the rondò was aimed at Laschi, since it seems likely that she and Storace were potentially in dispute over which sang the countess, and which Susanna.

42. Mozart did not revert to the 1786 sketch when Ferrarese required a rondò in 1789, perhaps because Figaro's aria is also in E flat. But that reasoning would imply that Mozart had not decided the key of Figaro's aria, though eventually it came to resemble the E flat aria for Bartolo in *Il barbiere di Siviglia*. Daniel Heartz and Thomas Bauman, *Mozart's Operas*, Berkeley and Los Angeles 1990, pp. 144–6; Rushton, 'Buffo roles in Mozart's Vienna', pp. 415–6.

43. In this concert she also sang her 'Scottish' aria from *Gli equivoci*, with German words. Link, *Arias for Nancy Storace*, p. xii.

herself.[44] But it was surely written to Nancy Storace's strengths, as the composer was her brother Stephen.

The rondò is the most elaborate formal type habitually used by Mozart in arias. Anyone singing a rondò is self-dramatizing. In *Gli equivoci* Sofronia's unmarried sister Sostrata also sings a rondò, 'A quei soavi detti', in F major. This is clearly intended to dramatize – to Sostrata herself, and to the audience – an erotic warming, for Sostrata has realised that she is falling in love with the man she believes is her sister's husband. The singer was almost certainly Laschi, and the rondò may have been included for a prima donna's reason: Laschi reportedly complained to the Burgtheater management that her role was inferior to Storace's.[45] But if this aria is inserted to placate the singer, it also develops the character – as does Elvira's 'Mi tradì quell'alma ingrata', added for Cavalieri in the Vienna *Don Giovanni*, and described by Kerman as 'thoroughly gratuitous'.[46] Elvira's and Sostrata's arias are both soliloquies, and *not* overheard by other characters. Both explore the projection of feelings onto what the singer believes is an unsuitable man. However, Elvira's aria is not a rondò; instead Mozart found his own musical metaphor for obsession, a seemingly endless circulation of modulating quaver figuration.

Thus, while we think of Nancy Storace as Susanna, she also aspired to sing the type of virtuoso aria so unsubtly mocked in *Der Schauspieldirektor*. The latter is not an opera; the vocal roles are not operatic characters but human singers. They were performed by Aloysia Lange and Cavalieri, both of whom returned to the opera buffa troupe in 1788 to sing Anna and Elvira in *Don*

44. Vitellia's 'Non più di fiori' is longer by a few bars, but its opening section is in short bars of 3/8, whereas Storace's opening section is in longer bars of 4/4. It is likely that 'Non tardar, amato bene' would have been shorter than 'Ah come in un istante'; Mozart broke off after the second statement of the slow theme in 35 bars, a point reached by Storace in 51 bars. For the Storace aria see *Gli equivoci, Musica Britannica* LXXXVI, pp. 106–114.

45. Link cites this gossip from Zinzendorf's diary in *The National Court Theatre*, p. 282. Laschi was paid about 75% of Storace's salary, but she was a newcomer that season. In her third and last season, during which she was pregnant but sang Zerlina, she equalled Storace's salary of 4500 (Link, op. cit., pp. 421, 430).

46. Kerman, *Opera as Drama* (1989 edition), p. 197.

Giovanni, while Laschi recreated Zerlina.[47] We may speculate, if Storace had still been in Vienna in 1788, which role in *Don Giovanni* she might have claimed: would she perhaps have chosen Donna Anna, the prima donna's role, with a final rondò? But Storace was atypical; partly responsible for creating the Susanna who sings 'Venite inginocchiatvi' and 'Deh vieni non tardar', she would surely have made a wonderful Zerlina. Zerlina seems modest compared to the other women, but she also dramatizes herself, most of all in 'Batti, batti' where, as Kerman puts it, she 'figuratively bares her backside'.[48] The contrast between the crudity of the words and beauty of the melody and cello obbligato affects the audience almost as much as it affects poor Masetto.

I must not create the impression that narcissistic self-dramatization is confined to women. *Così fan tutti* (sic): men do it too, and not only tenors. *Figaro* is again unusual because its tenor roles are purely comic. But Ferrando – Calvesi – is as prone to self-dramatization as his beloved Dorabella (or his beloved Fiordiligi). In 'Un aura amorosa' he develops a kind of erotic sermon, focused on his own responses. He forgets the mean trick he and Guglielmo are playing. His self-satisfied rondo 'Ah lo veggio' is routinely omitted (it may have been cut by Mozart). 'Tradito, schernito' dramatizes Ferrando's self-pity in a fashion denied to Guglielmo. Guglielmo, sung by Benucci, so pleased with himself in both his arias, before he has been betrayed, has no opportunity for a comparable display of egotism in the Act II finale: he mumbles his resentment under the canonic quartet. In fact he behaves like a real person, and sulks. But baritones can also self-dramatize. Unlike the Countess's arias, Count Almaviva's scena in Act III is based on Beaumarchais. In real life he would plot his revenge in grim silence. In the play he mutters disjointedly, then lays a plan, and exits:

> *Tu viens de gagner ton procès*! — je donnais là dans un bon piège! O mes chers insolents! .... Mais s'il allait payer la duègne... avec

47. Zerlina was sung in some performances by Therese Teyber, but Laschi played the role until immediately before her confinement and recovered it later.
48. Kerman, 'Reading *Don Giovanni*', p. 113.

> quoi? ... Eeeeh! N'ai-je pas le fier Antonio, dont le noble orgeuil dédaigne, en Figaro, un inconnu pour sa nièce? ... dans le vaste champ de l'intrigue, il faut savoir tout cultiver, jusqu'à la vanité d'un sot...[49]

In the opera this becomes recitative. The aria is added on, as, in Bernard Williams's words, an expression of 'the rage of baffled class power'.[50] Nothing could be more self-centred, even narcissistic; it is a quintessentially operatic exaggeration, and representative of opera at its most gloriously enjoyable. Perhaps the Count is one of those men most attractive when angry.

In the late eighteenth century, comic and serious genres of opera were increasingly permeable, one influencing the other. The kind of self-dramatization I have been discussing is perhaps more widespread in opera seria, and it occurs in reformist works by Gluck. In one scene of *Iphigénie en Tauride*, Oreste pretends to be mad, feigning a kind of epileptic fit, in order to win an argument; although his motives may seem altruistic, in that he is trying to allow Pylade to escape rather than himself, his main motive is that he wants to die, and dying on the Scythian altar will be a form of suicide, an act more often solipsistic than altruistic.[51] In *Idomeneo*, Idamante and Idomeneo self-dramatize as much as the women, and Sesto in *La clemenza di Tito* belongs to a long tradition of self-dramatizing castrati.

To say that operatic characters are normally self-absorbed, even narcissistic, is not an objection to opera. It is rather an attempt to celebrate opera as a unique form of drama. The penetration of music into our listening brains allows us an entry to the characters and their world in a way inaccessible to spoken drama: a way not necessarily better, but different. And finally, it suggests something about Don Giovanni himself. To be sure, he – the character within the fiction that is the opera – is psychologically flawed,

49. Beaumarchais, *Le mariage de Figaro*, Act III sc.11. Some of an earlier soliloquy (Act III sc.4–5), is overheard by Figaro.

50. Williams, *On Opera* , p. 37.

51. See Julian Rushton, '*Iphigénie en Tauride*: the Operas of Gluck and Piccinni', *Music and Letters*, 53 (1972), pp. 411-30.

selfish and narcissistic. We would probably not say as much about the other characters. But it is they who project their egos most powerfully to the audience, and to one another, especially in arias. This is musical narcissism: a grand aria, from Idomeneo, the Countess, Anna, Elvira, Fiordiligi – even the less haughty utterances of Susanna, Zerlina, or jealous Figaro in 'Aprite un po' quegli occhi' – says: 'LISTEN TO ME' – and by extension 'LOOK AT ME – *I* am the one that matters'. This is the egotistical syndrome satirized in *Der Schauspieldirektor*: 'Ich bin die erste Sängerin!'. It is self-dramatization writ larger than in any other dramatic form. Yet these are characters – the Countess, Anna, Elvira, Fiordiligi – that we rightly find sympathetic. 'Questo è il fin di chi fà mal': the moral is that in opera, a character like Don Giovanni, who is not 'musically' narcissistic, is one whom we – rightly – neither like nor trust.

DON OTTAVIO AND THE HISTORY OF THE TENOR VOICE[1]

Stefan Rohringer

I.
A 'DON OTTAVIO PROBLEM'?

Most scholars regard Don Ottavio as a problematic figure. Even those who are relatively well disposed toward him and see his lack of temperament as balanced by sincerity and rationality nevertheless concede that this trade-off has its limitations. Joachim Kaiser offers an insightful view:

> Don Ottavio is also surrounded by an air of restraint, of excessive gentility – all the more pronounced in a world of sexual predators and quick-tempered, vengeance-obsessed, eccentric characters. What he sorely lacks is resolute passion. That is why this nobleman, especially when his gracious ardor is expressed with even a little less forcefulness and intensity than as Mozart composed it, does not come across merely as an individual with strengths and weaknesses but often as someone who flimsily rationalizes, as it were – a bit of an oddball in the context of the impassioned story. The hotheads make the rational thinker look bad.[2]

---

1. I am very grateful to Michael Schubert, who translated this text from German into English, and to the University of Music and Performing Arts Munich, whose generous financial support made this translation possible.

2. 'So umgibt auch den Don Ottavio – zumal in einer Welt von Triebtätern, rasch Entflammten, Rachebesessenen und Exzentrischen – ein Air der Verhaltenheit, der allzu lieben Sanftheit. Allzusehr fehlt es ihm an entschiedener Leidenschaft. Darum wirkt dieser Edelmann, zumal wenn seine noble Gefühlsinnigkeit auch nur um ein weniges schwächer, unintensiver zum Ausdruck kommt, als Mozart sie komponiert hat, nicht nur wie ein spezifischer Mensch mit Vorzügen und Schwächen, sondern oft gleichsam dürr-vernüftelnd, ja im Kontext der glühenden Handlung ein wenig komisch. Die Rasenden blamieren den Rationalen.' Joachim Kaiser, *Who's Who in Mozarts Meisteropern*, Munich & Zürich: Pieper, 1997, p. 196.

But those who – like Adorno, writing mockingly of the 'groom of all grooms'[3] – see the figure as approaching or even going beyond the ridiculous, need more than 'gentility' and 'reason' to see Ottavio as honorable. Wolfgang Hildesheimer put it this way: 'Nothing can quite reconcile us to the figure of Don Ottavio. We do not see this unimaginative, virtuous young man as the husband of a domineering and passionate girl.'[4]

The low level of interest that Ottavio is generally afforded is ultimately reflected in the dearth of research dedicated to the role's finer points. However, there have been occasional attempts to solve the 'Don Ottavio problem' – or 'alleged problem,' to put it more aptly – even with radical suggestions. One such attempt comes from Christian Rault[5], whose essay 'Don Ottavio, ténor de circonstance' offers up the question: 'And what would happen if a courageous stage director teamed up with an understanding artistic director and decided to leave out the two tenor arias?'[6]

Rault is of the opinion that Mozart, in composing the two arias, was merely following a convention that departs from the 'true nature' of the figure: 'The development of Don Ottavio is actually so closely linked to that of Donna Anna and her vengeance that, dramatically speaking, he lacks the time (and the need) to turn inward.'[7] Of 'Il mio tesoro', Rault writes: 'If it is his intention during the second act to run off and alert the police (a logical and reasonable sentiment), then the point of this is most certainly not to [then afterward] sing 'Il mio

3. 'Bräutigam aller Bräutigamme' Theodor W. Adorno, 'Klemperers' "Don Giovanni, *Gesammelte Schriften*", edited by Rolf Tiedemann, Vol. 19 (1997), pp. 539–544, p. 543.
4. 'Des Don Ottavio werden wir auch sonst nicht recht froh. Dieses phantasiearme tugendhafte Herrchen sehen wir nicht als Gatten eines herrischen und leidenschaftlichen Mädchens.' Wolfgang Hildesheimer, *Mozart*, Frankfurt a.M.: Suhrkamp, 1980, p. 235.
5. My thanks to Konstantin Esterl, whose translation into German made it possible for me to familiarize myself with Rault's text.
6. 'Et si un metteur en scène courageux doublé d'un chef compréhensif décidaient de supprimer les deux airs du ténor?' Christian Rault, 'Don Ottavio, ténor de circonstance,' *Musical: Revue du Théâtre Musical de Paris-Châtelet,* 1/1987, pp. 89–93, p. 89.
7. 'L'évolution de Don Ottavio est, en effet, si liée à celle de Donna Anna et à sa vengeance que ce personnage n'a pour ainsi dire dramatiquement pas le temps – ni la nécessité – de se pencher sur lui-même.' Ibid., p. 92 f.

tesoro!'[8] And of 'Dalla sua pace', Rault writes: 'What a context for 'Dalla sua pace'! Right after 'Or sai chi l'onore' – in which Donna Anna sweeps us up into a world of passion where we might also expect to find Don Ottavio, judging from the earlier vengeance duet – this romance stands out for the inexplicable manner in which it breaks the tone.'[9]

No question about it: Rault notes the contrast that exists between Donna Anna's demand for vengeance and Don Ottavio's restraint as expressed in his arias.[10] But the primary reason why Rault's ideas raise objections, aside from the pressing question as to whether he has been overly naïve in the friendly colours with which he portrays the role of Don Ottavio alongside Donna Anna, is that the characteristics attributed to Don Ottavio are consistently apparent: the 'favourable' qualities cannot simply be assigned to the Ottavio of the recitatives and ensembles and the 'unfavourable' to the Ottavio of the arias. Implementing Rault's suggestion would therefore by no means yield greater cohesion in the character of Don Ottavio. Three examples illustrate this:

a. The first and last scenes of Don Ottavio in *Don Giovanni* have something in common: Don Ottavio arrives too late. At the end of the opera, it is not earthly justice dispensed by Don Ottavio, but the heavenly variety that is visited upon Don Giovanni;

---

8. 'Si, au cours du IIe acte, il se précipite pur aller prévenir la police (attitude logique et sensée), ce n'est certainement pas pour chanter 'Il mio tesoro!" Ibid. p. 93.

9. 'A quoi correspond en effet ce 'Dalla sua pace'! Située immédiatement après 'Or sai chi l'onore' où Donna Anna nous entraîne dans l'univers passionnel et dans lequel, à la suite du duo de la vengeance, nous sommes en droit d'associer Don Ottavio, cette romance détonne par son inexplicable rupture de ton.' Ibid.

10. A more differentiated analysis would of course reveal that there are important differences between the two arias. Unfortunately, there is a tradition of the largely undifferentiated examination of the two arias that we see with Rault. Hermann Killer (cf. Note 40) was also unable to see any significant difference in the basic affect of the two arias: 'Il mio tesoro' was, in his view, 'largely a lyric love song despite the reference to vengeance', Hermann Killer, *Die Tenorpartien in Mozarts Opern. Ein Beitrag zur Geschichte und Stil des Bühnengesangs*, Kassel: Bärenreiter, 1929, p. 61. See also Shirley Trembath, 'Mozart's operatic characterizations: Musical factors,' *Internationaler Musikwissenschaftlicher Kongreß zum Mozartjahr 1991, Baden-Wien*, edited by Ingrid Fuchs, Tutzing: Schneider, 1993, pp. 979–99, and the related discussion below in the main text.

while at the start of the opera, Don Ottavio misses the opportunity to either confront the dishonorable stranger who has entered the chambers of his betrothed, or to intervene in the ensuing duel and prevent the death of the Commendatore. A small detail, inconspicuous at first, attracts our attention here: 'Ah soccorrete, amici, il mio tesoro!'[11] are Don Ottavio's words to those present when Donna Anna, discovering the body of her father, is on the verge of fainting. At its core, this anticipates the sentiment of the first verse of his aria 'Il mio tesoro', except that here it's about smelling salts, not the emotional support referred to later in the aria. Nevertheless, the episode portrays Don Ottavio as someone who is apparently accustomed to letting other people do things for him rather than taking matters into his own hands – even when it comes to the minor details of life. So it seems disconcerting when Don Ottavio shows us what is apparently an entirely different side of himself, not even stopping at blatant indiscretions: first, he tries to have the slain Commendatore quickly removed, ostensibly to protect Donna Anna. But then, in their duet together, another motivation is revealed. Responding to Donna Anna's question as to the whereabouts of her father, Don Ottavio sings: 'Il padre ... lascia, o cara, / La rimembranza amara ... / Hai sposo e padre in me'.[12]

Ulrich Schulz-Buschhaus used this scene as the basis for portraying Don Ottavio as a symbol of bourgeois gender identity: 'He is exemplary in his willingness to respect the specific bourgeois duality of 'sposa' and 'amica' in his future wife. This means that he himself is also willing to take on the combined responsibilities of spouse and lover – 'E di sposo e d'amico/ Il dover.' [...] And at one point he even announces his desire – carried away by a sort of familial exuberance that counteracts Don Giovanni's

11. 'Oh hurry, my friends, and help my beloved!'
12. 'Your father? Banish, my dear, the bitter memory. You have a husband and father in me.'

libertine 'excesses' – to fulfill for Donna Anna all key masculine family functions at the same time.'[13]

But even if we are accustomed to spans of time generally unfolding more rapidly in operas than in real life, the haste with which Don Ottavio seeks to fill the role of the Commendatore not only shows a disconcerting lack of respect toward the murder victim, whose corpse is not even cold yet, but also disregards Donna Anna's right to mourn her father fully. It seems reasonable to assume that the rivalry evident here between the Commendatore and Don Ottavio had defined the relationship of both men to Donna Anna even before the events of that fateful night. What's obvious in any event is that the limits of empathy, which Don Ottavio is generally considered to embody[14], are finally reached when they collide with Oedipal rituals of masculinity.

b. The only direct confrontation between Don Ottavio and Don Giovanni that offers an opportunity for revenge takes place in the finale of Act I. The stage directions here indicate that Don Ottavio has since exchanged the sword he drew in his first scene for a pistol. This nondescript prop distinguishes Don Ottavio as a 'man of the future'[15] from Don Giovanni as a representative of the *ancien régime*: the firearm represents modernity. As a long-distance weapon, it circumvents the need for a one-on-one sword fight. It becomes possible to evade direct physical and psychological

13. 'So ist er vorbildlich bereit, in der künftigen Gattin die spezifisch bürgerliche Personalunion von 'sposa' und 'amica' zu respektieren, was bedeutet, dass auch er selbst bereitwillig die vereinten Pflichten des Gatten und des Liebhabers – 'E di sposo e d'amico/ Il dover' – auf sich nimmt. [...] Und einmal kündigt er – von einer Art familialistischem Überschwang, der Don Giovannis libertinistische 'Exzesse' konterkariert, hingerissen – sogar an, gegenüber Donna Anna alle wesentlichen maskulinen Familienfunktionen gleichzeitig erfüllen zu wollen.' Ulrich Schulz-Buschhaus, 'Don Giovanni oder die Wandlungen eines Libertin,' *Mozarts Opernfiguren. Grosse Herren, rasende Weiber – gefährliche Liebschaften*, edited by Dieter Borchmeyer; Bern, Stuttgart & Vienna: Paul Haupt, pp. 71–91, p. 90.

14. 'Compassionate sympathy and support are what characterize Don Ottavio, and that is not unimportant [Empfindende Teilnahme, Beistand ist Don Ottavios Sache – und das ist nicht wenig].' Stefan Kunze, *Mozarts Opern*, Stuttgart: Reclam, 1984, p. 425.

15. 'Mann der Zukunft' Friedrich Dieckmann, *Die Geschichte Don Giovannis. Werdegang eines erotischen Anarchisten*, Frankfurt a.M. & Leipzig: Insel, 1991, p. 336.

confrontation with the opponent, compensating for one's own physical and mental inferiority. Even so, Don Ottavio is incapable of exploiting this advantage. Don Giovanni escapes.[16]

A pistol seems to be the right weapon to take a suspect into custody; it is the weapon *par excellence* of state authority. This anticipates the motive that Don Ottavio will reveal only in his address in Act II, Scene X: '... un ricorso / Vo' far a chi si deve, e in pochi instanti / Vendicarvi prometto.'[17] Schulze-Buschhaus also interpreted this passage in the sense of Don Ottavio as the 'model citizen,'[18] who 'quite properly [appeals] to the authorities because – in strikingly stark contrast to Don Giovanni – he has already accepted it as natural that the state (enlightened and absolutist in this case) should have a monopoly on power.'[19]

But Don Ottavio, despite the avowal in his subsequent aria 'Il mio tesoro' not to return except as the messenger of bloody vengeance, appears next at the side of Donna Anna once again with only the mere prospect of revenge. We do not know whether Don Ottavio had already been to see the 'authorities,' but in any event, he will appear even in the *scena ultima* without any police in attendance. He always seems to be thinking ahead to the next step, putting off the task at hand. And so we see a repeat of the situation immediately following the murder of the Commendatore, with Don Ottavio again offering himself as a father figure to Donna Anna: 'Di tua perdita amara Fia domani, se vuoi, dolce compenso / Questo cor, questo mano ... / Che il mio tenero

16. The libretto's directions provide no enlightenment as to why Don Giovanni manages to escape – and the explanations offered by most stagings come off as clumsy or far-fetched as one would expect. It seems to be Don Giovanni's mental imperturbability alone that makes him physically invulnerable – at least for his worldly foes.

17. 'I will appeal to the authorities for help, and I promise you that vengeance will soon be served.'

18. 'Modellbürger' Schulz-Buschhaus 1991, p. 89.

19. 'Selbst in der Oper rekurriert er als Modellbürger, wie es sich gehört, auf die zuständigen Behörden, da ihm – in plakativ scharfem Gegensatz zu Don Giovanni – das Gewaltmonopol des (hier aufgeklärt absolutistischen) Staates bereits zur Selbstverständlichkeit geworden ist.' Ibid.

amor …'[20] Only now do we see the reaction of incredulity that we would not have begrudged Donna Anna in the parallel scene but which did not manifest itself, likely due to her helpless state of shock: 'Oh Dei, che dite? … / In sì tristi momenti …'[21] For the first and only time, Don Ottavio protests: 'E che? vorrest / Con indugi novelli / Accrescer le mie pene? Crudele!'[22] Donna Anna replies by taking her leave – and giving him his: 'Tu ben sai quant'io t'amai.'[23] Note the use of the past tense to represent something that has already come to an end!

c. 'Otherwise, he is a methodical man of both cautious and persistent efficiency who, despite the love to which the music so beautifully attests, does not allow Anna to draw him into the web of excitability to which she – along with her father – has just fallen victim. Before he accepts what his quick-tempered bride-to-be believes to be true, he wants proof, and he goes about gathering it step by step – a perfect bureaucrat.'[24] Friedrich Dieckman is mistaken: In the vengeance duet, right at the beginning of his thread of the plot, Don Ottavio has allowed himself to be drawn utterly into the 'web' of Donna Anna's excitability. And his oath to exact revenge is what dogs him for the rest of the opera. He feels it from the start: 'Fra cento affeti e cento / Vammi ondeggiando il cor.'[25]

Don Ottavio's search for more and more proof, even when everything is already proven, has an air of making excuses: if this man is a bureaucrat, then it's because he senses he's not up to the task he signed on for. Even his reaction to Donna Anna's renewed call for vengeance in her aria 'Or sai chi l'onore' is surprising, given

20. 'Tomorrow, if you desire, you shall find sweet compensation for your bitter loss with this heart, this hand … my tender love …'
21. 'Oh God, what are you saying? … At such a sad time …'
22. 'What? Would you increase my agony with further delay? Cruel woman!'
23. 'You know full well how I loved you.'
24. 'Im übrigen ist er ein Methodiker von ebenso vorsichtiger wie zäher Effizienz, der sich, bei aller Liebe, die die Musik ihm arios konzediert, von Anna nicht ins Schlepptau jener Erregbarkeit nehmen läßt, der diese – mit ihrem Vater – ja gerade zum Opfer gefallen ist. Ehe er annimmt, was seine hitzige Anverlobte für wahr hält, will er Beweise haben und sammelt sie, ein perfekter Bürokrat, Schritt um Schritt.' Dieckmann, p. 336.
25. 'My heart is tossed about between countless emotions.'

the fact that Donna Anna has already identified Don Giovanni as the offender: 'Disingannarla voglio, o vendicarla.'[26] What type of evidence does Don Ottavio seek to bring for or against Don Giovanni? After Donna Anna has told the story of her nocturnal encounter, what more is there that could offer further insight?

Part of what makes Mozart and Da Ponte's work so compelling is that in Don Ottavio, they have created a figure in which naïveté and repression are balanced without precluding each other. That does not always suit those whose judgment is guided by the expectation of a more sophisticated personality development, so they suspect intent. This is why Hildesheimer interprets the exclamation 'Ohime respiro'[27] (no. 10, bars 52 f.) – Don Ottavio's response to Donna Anna's account of the nocturnal visit of Don Giovanni – 'as a *Trugschluss* […], as if he [Don Ottavio] – having assured himself of her [Donna Anna's] virtue – does not wish to hear anything that could call it into doubt again.'[28]

But is it not almost a misinterpretation of the musical syntax to assert that it is Don Ottavio who interrupts the regular flow of the music? In the typical manner of the recitative, Donna Anna finishes her statement before the music itself comes to an end (bar 51). Despite the positive ending of the text ('Da lui mi sciolsi'[29]), the music moves toward a cadence in A minor, leading the listener to expect a negative end to the story. If the end of Donna Anna's narrative comes as a surprise – and one may call it a surprise that a woman manages unassisted to free herself from a stronger man – then the uplifting move to F major (bar 52) can be called

26. 'I will disprove her suspicions – or avenge them.'
27. 'Oh, I can breathe again!'
28. ‚[…] wo er [Don Ottavio] dem atemlosen, vor allem für ihn reichlich spät kommenden Moll-Bericht der Angebeteten mit seinem Dur-Ausruf 'Ohimé, respiro' einen Trugschluß zu setzen scheint, als wolle er, nachdem er sich von der Tugend [Donna Annas] überzeugt habe, nichts mehr hören, das sie noch in Zweifel ziehen könnte.' Hildesheimer 1980, p. 235.
29. '... freed myself of him.'

its musical counterpart.[30] In exclaiming his relief on the newly achieved harmonic level, Don Ottavio is of course only embracing that which Donna Anna 'says' on the literal level while missing the subliminal dimension that her narrative 'shows', and with this, also the consequence that this inevitably has for their relationship: for irrespective of the question of whether or not there was any physical contact with Don Giovanni, the events of the night certainly constitute a profound sexual experience on the part of Donna Anna which, despite the negative context of attempted rape and the murder of her father, binds her to Don Giovanni.

So we cannot prove that Don Ottavio is intentionally suppressing, but neither can we say for certain what the limits of his naïveté are. The only explanation for Donna Elvira, Donna Anna and Don Ottavio's visit to the ball of Don Giovanni at the end of Act I is their intention to either take their vengeance on Don Giovanni then and there or, at the very least, confront him. And even if Don Ottavio still needed the incident with Zerlina to convince him that Don Giovanni is the nocturnal stranger and murderer of the Commendatore whom they all seek, Don Ottavio shows unmistakably that he is convinced of Don Giovanni's guilt when he shouts 'Nol sperate!'[31] at Don Giovanni as the latter tries to finger Leporello as Zerlina's seducer. Or is Don Ottavio's utterance directed only at Don Giovanni's assault on Zerlina and does he actually believe that this does not also show him to be guilty of the assault on Donna Anna and the murder of the Commendatore as well? Should we accept what he said in direct response to Donna Anna's account – 'Come mai creder deggio /

30. It is important to call to mind that Hildesheimer's interpretation depends heavily on the potential 'metaphorical exemplification' (Nelson Goodman) in the word *Trugschluss* – a Germanized form of the Italian *cadenza d'inganno* (deceptive cadence) – while the suggestion here is to assume the *ausgeflohene Kadenz*, which corresponds to the Italian *cadenza sfuggita* ('interrupted' or 'avoided' cadence). In this context, it seems not at all insignificant that historically, the term *Trugschluss* for the V-vi progression came later and was adopted consistently into common usage only after 1800 (cf. Michael Beiche 'Fuga / Fuge,' *Terminologie der musikalischen Komposition*, edited by Hans Heinrich Eggebrecht, Stuttgart: Steiner, 1996, p. 103–144, p. 106).
31. 'It's useless!' [i.e., Don Giovanni's deception]

Di si nero delitto / Capace un Cavaliere!'[32] – as the prophesy of an irreversible conviction?

In the context of these events in the finale to Act I, it is downright confounding in Act II, Scene X, when – after everyone has initially fallen prey to the charade perpetrated by Don Giovanni and Leporello – Don Ottavio turns to those assembled and announces that he has now determined Don Giovanni to be the man they are seeking: 'Amici miei, / Dopo eccessi si enormi / Dubitar non possimam che Don Giovanni / Non sia l'empio uccisore / Del padre di Donn'Anna.'[33] Aside from the fact that, strictly speaking, no proof has actually been provided for Don Giovanni's guilt even now, Don Ottavio seems to believe that he must convince the other pursuers of his newly formed opinion. Is such a disconnection from reality possible, or is someone trying to excuse his failure to act earlier by pretending that this is a new insight?

No, simply cutting out Don Ottavio's two arias does nothing whatsoever to erase the inconsistencies in his character. He embodies a deep-seated contradiction that winds through the entire plot. The evident inhibition, in which rationality serves to excuse passivity, is contrasted by a self-assessment that extends far beyond his own potential and is permeated by latent hubris. One has the impression that Don Ottavio's behaviour is forced, especially when his actions are directed at Donna Anna or his other companions. One can see this as an attempt bordering on the embarrassing to block out his own weakness and sense of impotence. Without question, this is no less an articulation of the desire to finally find his own position, to perform a role.

'Role' – that is the critical word, for a conflict like that of Don Ottavio is not yet grasped in its entire dimension if the figure that endures it is seen only as the expression of a sociopolitical situation and thus as the documentation of a time in history (as Schulze-Buschhaus sees it) or is measured solely against the standards of a fully developed individual psychology and thus forever against the motivations of modern reality of life (Rault,

32. 'How could I ever believe a nobleman capable of so black a crime?'
33. 'My friends, after such gross excesses we can no longer doubt that Don Giovanni is the villainous murderer of Donna Anna's father.'

Hildesheimer). Both approaches, in their abstraction, lose sight of the fact that an operatic figure is not ultimately a real person – not in history and not in the present – but primarily a character in a fictional space: that of the stage. What's overlooked in the process is that such figures, through their association with various voice types, are rooted in the historical development of the genre. But it is only with the background of this historical dimensioning that the conflicts suffered by the figures develop their actual depth. The sediment of the voice genre's history becomes a millstone to all attempts to give a particular figure a new accent, and this millstone grinds down such attempts, as it were. So it would be problematic in terms of conventional stylistic criticism to assume that Mozart's figures merely moved away from a general background through individualization. What actually distinguishes Mozart's figures is that they render the topological comprehensible to begin with. Even as singular figures they are bound by a functionality in which the general is not simply reshaped through individualization but remains recognizable as the actual force behind the character development.

What distinguishes the work of Mozart and Da Ponte from that of their contemporaries is the keen awareness the two had of the traditions that are the necessary bedrock of a convincing renewal of any role type. The extensive knowledge that both artists possessed of the literary and musical methods of their predecessors is not merely the prerequisite to giving nuance to, modifying or reinventing role types, it is also reflected in the fictional space of the stage action itself: Mozart and Da Ponte's cast of characters often consist of figures who are evolving in various ways, searching for their own identity – usually on the threshold between youth and adulthood. They pass through an 'initiation' in the course of the opera.[34] Only here do we find the roots of the deeper motivation for a reflection of the role typology: The examination of the traditional understanding of the role appears

34. Of course, it is precisely this all-important relationship that is often rendered indiscernible on the stage by questionable casting decisions.

in the process of self-discovery to be 'inserted' into the individual figure, as it were.

2. THE TENOR VOICE – ITS HISTORY AND RENEWAL WITH MOZART

The above observations are especially true of the tenors in Mozart and Da Ponte's operas, because the tenor had undergone a varied history like almost no other voice type and thus offered a great potential for development in the renewal process.

From the earliest history of opera, voices have been associated with role characters based on the character of their tone. In Italian opera, the tenor has been featured since the early 17th century in the male lead as the youthful hero and lover: Orfeo in the *Euridice* operas of Caccini and Peri (both from 1600), in Monteverdi's *Orfeo* (1607), and in *Egisto* (1643) and *Ormindo* (1644) by Francesco Cavalli. After Monteverdi, the tendency is established to use a soprano voice for the gods and a low bass voice for demons, magicians and sorcerers. In general, youth is portrayed with a high voice, age and dignity with a low voice.[35]

In the tenor voice, the youthful hero and lover are at first inextricably linked: only the active figure who overcomes every type of obstacle can possess the (sexual) potency that explains success as a lover. This coupling even remains intact around the mid 17th century as the tenor increasingly loses its role as the leading male voice to the rapidly ascending castrati. Though Pope Sixtus VI

35. In the ensuing period, the bass voice becomes increasingly unimportant in Italy in favor of an independent youth tolerated by the gods – unlike in Germany and France, where the bass retains its demonic associations. One example is the figure of the sorcerer Seneca in Monteverdi's *L'incoronazione di Poppea*, 'whose wisdom has been reduced to sententiousness, authority to a hoary-headed posturing' See Roger Covell, 'Voice register as an index of age and status in opera seria,' *Opera & Vivaldi*, edited by Michael Collins and Elise K. Kirk, Austin TX: University of Texas, 1986, pp. 193–210, p. 195.

had condemned castration in 1587, the first documentation of a castrato in the papal chapel choir is from the very next year.[36]

The rise of the castrati initially benefited from the limited opportunities offered to women to take part in opera productions: a papal decree of 1588 prohibited women from working in theaters within the city of Rome. Here, however, less effort was expended to circumvent the papal orders. Though there were discussions on relaxing the ban – prompted, for example, by Domenico Mazzocchi's opera *La Catena d'Adone* (1626) – the fear of scandal prevailed: the two roles intended for women were ultimately cast with castrati from the papal chapel.[37]

But the fact that castrati not only filled the roles of women but also penetrated the domain of male roles, where they soon proved to be the only singers capable of handling the enormous technical challenges of the virtuoso roles, illustrates that their rise was much more than an emergency solution. This trend originated primarily in a system of aesthetics in which the hierarchy among the figures was depicted directly in the voice types: the social status and even (sexual) potency of a figure is revealed by his ability to rise above the other figures in vocal pitch.

Add to this the special timbre of the castrato voice – an aspect strongly underscored by the content of the libretti, which generally involved mythical scenarios populated with a tumultuous cast of ancient demigods, generals and their ilk:

> The aim was not to depict reality but to transport theatergoers into imaginary worlds. An inhuman voice – seemingly disembodied – that

---

36. Immediately, there were attempts to explain the discrepancy between policy and reality, primarily through myths about the origin of the disfiguration: not surgery but accidents of all sorts – overturned carriages, biting pigs, runaway horses and so forth – were put forward to explain the castrations.

37. 'In principle, these bans only applied to Rome and the papal state, but in general, they strengthened moral objections to women performing in public, even in places where the bans were not in effect [Diese Verbote galten im Prinzip nur für Rom und den Kirchenstaat, doch im Allgemeinen bestärkten die Singverbote auch dort, wo sie keine direkte Gültigkeit hatten, moralische Bedenken gegen den öffentlichen Auftritt von Frauen].' See Birthe Schwarz 'Das Spiel mit den Geschlechterrollen. Kastraten und Primadonnen im Musiktheater des 18. Jahrhunderts,' *Gender Studies & Musik. Geschlechterrollen und ihre Bedeutung für die Musikwissenschaft*, Regensburg: Con Brio, 1998, pp. 75–84, here: p. 76.

> dispatched the most difficult vocal passages without any apparent effort gave the impression of encountering a living demigod upon the stage.[38]

During the heyday of the castrati, the tenor often had to be content to play a secondary role as the advisor or (unlucky) opponent of the young hero and lover[39], but the Enlightenment of the mid 18th century brought about yet another shift in the understanding of the tenor role. The new view of nature stood in stark contrast to the unnatural art of the castrati. The dictate of naturalness and veracity in how roles were conceived – think of Gluck's reform of opera – led at least in part to the subordination of the singers' ambitions to the dramatic intentions of the librettist and composer, enabling an innovative individualization of the vocal part. The result was not simply a restoration of the original identity of the tenor from the time before the golden age of the castrati but a splintering of the various characteristics among the various types of roles and voices.

As Hermann Killer wrote, in what remains the only study dedicated to the tenor parts in Mozart's operas[40], 'the role of the hero split off from that of the lover.'[41] Here, Killer describes a distinction among the *opere serie* that was to remain characteristic for Mozart into the works of his mature period: 'The hero, usually a military personality – emperor, general, etc. – is increasingly

38. 'Es wurde keine Realität abgebildet, sondern in Phantasiewelten entführt. Durch eine nichtmenschliche Stimme, die – wie vom Körper gelöst – scheinbar mühelos schwierigste Gesangspassagen darbot, entstand der Eindruck, auf der Bühne einem leibhaftigen Halbgott zu begegnen.' Ibid., p. 77.

39. 'The tenor voice, which was initially used to portray even younger gods, had to make do in the role of advisors, even traitors [Die Tenorstimme, der zu Beginn auch jüngere Götter anvertraut wurden, musste sich später mit Ratgebern, aber auch Verrätern begnügen].' See Bernd Göpfert, *Handbuch der Gesangskunst*, Wilhelmshaven: Noetzel, 2002, p. 153.

40. Unfortunately, Killer's treatise (1929) suffers from a pronounced nationalistic tone, in which Mozart's works are used first and foremost to illustrate the creation of a 'German' position that distances itself from the Italian and above all French operatic styles. Killer takes an approach that was typical for Mozart research in the years between the World Wars. This same position can be found, for example, in Hermann Abert's earlier biography of Mozart (1990), which was first published in 1920. Accordingly, Killer uses the tenor part of Tamino to shore up his arguments.

41. '[Es] sondert sich das Fach des Helden von dem des Liebhabers.' Killer 1929, p. 11.

portrayed by the tenor [...], while the primary lover, whose hallmark traits are youth and gentle passion, remains the domain of the castrati.'[42] And so even then the tenor is not considered for the role of the successful lover in the *opera seria*. The reason lies in the continued association of erotic success with vocal register: 'The tenor, as the lowest voice in the *opera seria*, cannot be the lover.'[43] And so Mozart continues to cast a castrato in the role of the lover in all his *opere serie* (Ascanio, Farnace, Idamante[44] and Sesto) while casting a tenor in the title roles and the roles of fathers and kings (Mitridate, Lucio Silla, Idomeneo and Titus).

The reassessment of the tenor voice thus transpires not in *opera seria* but in *Singspiel* and *opera buffa*. Only here, where castrati were typically unwelcome, was the tenor able to find his way back into the role of the successful lover. Mozart's second *opera buffa* – *La finta giardiniera* (1775) – can be regarded as a transitional work in this regard. As the designation *dramma giocoso* already suggests, it integrates moments of *opera seria*, making it an *opera semiseria*: the three high male voices include not only the original *buffo* tenor part of Podestà but the mezzo character of Belfiore and the *seria* role of Ramiro, intended for a castrato but with a whiff of parody through its contextualization in the *buffo* storyline.

But even after the castrato finally abdicated its role of the rival to the tenor, the restitution of the tenor as the successful lover is impeded by the dramaturgical concept of the *buffo*. Where the *seria* uses guilt and entanglement to advance the plot, *opera buffa* relies on comedic intrigues in the tradition of the *commedia dell'arte*. This explains the importance of the ensemble in the very place best suited for displaying the temporary confusion of all protagonists, and it is not surprising that the tenor initially re-establishes itself as an ensemble singer. The dramaturgical

42. 'Der Held, meistens eine kriegerische Persönlichkeit: Kaiser, Feldherr usw. fällt immer mehr dem Tenor zu [...]. Dagegen bleibt der ausgesprochene Liebhaber, dessen Eigenschaften vor allem Jugend und weiche Schwärmerei sind, nach wie vor dem Kastraten vorbehalten.' Ibid.

43. Ibid. At this point, *opera seria* does not yet include the voice type known later as *basso serio*.

44. Mozart rewrote the part for tenor for a concert performance in Vienna in 1786.

concept of the *opera buffa* and *Singspiel*, on the other hand, does not offer the tenor any real opportunity for character development as the *primo uomo*, for the hallmark of character development in the *buffo* is 'reversing the polarity'[45] of the *seria*. Heroic tasks are not usually called for, and when they are, as in *Die Entführung aus dem Serail,* where it is Belmonte's intention to abduct Konstanze – a plot that stems primarily from the similarity of *Singspiel* to stage plays – the stronger dramatic momentum still lies typically with the *buffo* character – as here with Perdrillio. Belmonte, on the other hand, gives himself over primarily to his feelings. Across long stretches of the plot, he seems to be less involved in realizing his plan than with his own feelings – especially with his (not-so-friendly) speculations about Konstanze's faithfulness. In this situation the tenor risks the same fate as the castrato Ramiro in *La finta giardiniera*: he seems to be passive, especially in the context of the disclosure of his own emotional world. In the light of his weak social skills and his stereotypical behaviour he appears to be slightly autistic.[46]

Which brings us to Don Ottavio. Now we see that his inhibition can be traced back to the separation of the hero from the lover. His conflict seems all the more tragic when Don Ottavio – who like Donna Anna is conceived as a *seria* character as a result of the dramaturgical concept that in *Don Giovanni*, as a *dramma giocoso*, combines plot elements of *buffo* and *seria* – does not lack opportunities for heroism in his pursuit of Don Giovanni. Nor is there any question that Don Ottavio tries to restore the old congruity of hero and lover. He knows: this is the only way he will find success in the affairs of the heart, and so Don Ottavio comes up against the recent history of his vocal genre. Now, with the

45. 'Umkehrung der Vorzeichen' in Martin Kunath, 'Die Charakterologie der stimmlichen Einheiten der Oper,' *Deutsche Musikgesellschaft. Zeitschrift für Musikwissenschaft*, 8/1925/26, pp. 403–410, p. 405.

46. This also leads to the alienation felt upon closer examination of Tamino's trials, for example: here the plot dictates a drama that hardly conforms with Tamino's image as strictly a lover and not a hero. (It is not he but the three ladies who kill the dragon.) The end of the opera therefore fails to live up to the expectations that the scene initially motivates: the premature appearance of Pamina and the opportunity for a love duet that it opens up blunts the effect of the ostensibly dramatic situation.

abdication of the castrato, the stage seems finally to be cleared for him to assume his original role as the *primo uomo* and, at the end of the opera – in the inimitable words of Bernd Göpfert – take 'rightful possession of his soprano partner.'[47] But then something unexpected happens: The ascent of a new voice type – the baritone – dashes all the hopes of our tenor.

This new turn of events is unquestionably due to the altered view of the natural order: the lower register identifies the baritone as the figure with the greater experience in matters of love.[48] Though the baritone does not ultimately succeed in restoring the old congruity of hero and lover, his physical-erotic presence is enough to thwart the tenor in his own ambitions – even from beyond the grave, as the example of *Don Giovanni* shows.

This confrontation between tenor and baritone seems to be specific to the characters in Mozart and Da Ponte's work, however. This can be seen by comparing 'Il dissoluto punito ossia il Don Giovanni' with its immediate predecessor, 'Don Giovanni Tenorio, o sia Il convitato di pietra' by Gazzaniga and Bertati (also from 1787). The same picture emerges when comparing 'Le nozze di Figaro' (1786) and 'Il barbiere di Siviglia, ovvero La precauzione inutile' (1782) by Paisiello and Petrosellini: Gazzaniga and Bertati cast not only Duca Ottavio as a tenor but also Don Giovanni, who is even permitted to sing a veritable love song ('Per voi nemmeno in faccia'). And Paisiello and Petrosellini pair the baritone Figaro with a lyric tenor for 'Il conte Almaviva', who at the work's end even prevails as a lover.

Not so with Don Ottavio: as much as he tries to escape the shadow of history, he doesn't get past oaths and pronouncements. The passions of love do not serve to compensate his inactivity: 'He is the type of beautifully singing tenor who does not initiate any dramatic action or undergo any critical development […] but remains in the end what he was at the beginning and always

47. 'Allerdings ist er am Ende meist glücklicher, nämlich in rechtmäßigem Besitz seiner Sopranpartnerin.' Göpfert 2002, 164 ff.

48. This is not synonymous with a higher biological age, as can be seen in the example of Don Giovanni, who after all is not an ageing Casanova but rather synonymous with a higher biological age, 'giovane cavaliere estremamente licenzioso'.

had been.'[49] The role of Don Ottavio magnifies the antagonism of the waning 18th century between the traditions of the tenor role on the one hand and its renewal on the other.

Rault, in referring to the 'two tenor arias,'[50] recalls today's common theatrical practice of performing both 'Il mio tesoro' and 'Dalla sua pace' in one performance. This became possible because Mozart placed 'Dalla sua pace', which had been added for the Vienna performances, in a different part of the opera than the original Prague aria 'Il mio tesoro'. Not only does the source material offer no conclusive evidence that Mozart and Da Ponte meant the new aria to supplement rather than replace the original Prague aria[51], but also our very outline of the history of the tenor voice illustrates that the presentation of both arias is based on entirely questionable premises, even from a textual perspective. This is because the distinction between *primo uomo* and a secondary role is marked – as we have seen – by success in matters of love. But as we can see by the end of *Don Giovanni*, if not earlier, Don Ottavio is not afforded this success, and it is precisely for this reason that he is conceived as a secondary role. So in creating the roles as they did, Mozart and Da Ponte remain entirely within the realm of convention. The break with convention that is nevertheless undoubtedly present is only revealed when the opera is regarded in its entirety: it comes about precisely because the 'downgrade' of Don Ottavio leaves the position of the traditional *primo uomo* unfilled. This point is thwarted, of course, if both of Don Ottavio's arias are presented – too much for his profile as a secondary role.

---

49. 'Er ist der Typ des schönsingenden Tenors, von dem keine dramatischen Impulse ausgehen, der keine entscheidende Entwicklung durchmacht, [...] sondern am Ende das ist, was er am Anfang und schon immer war.' Göpfert, Ibid.

50. Cf. Note 6.

51. As Rehm's discussion (2003) of the source material shows, it can be regarded as highly improbable that any such performance took place during Mozart's life – or that Mozart wished to suggest such a decision with his placement of 'Dalla sua pace'. Nevertheless, it became common theatrical practice to perform both arias, and 'Il mio tesoro' is not typically cut even when the third aria of Donna Elvira is included. See Wolfgang Rehm, *Kritischer Bericht zu Don Giovanni*, NMA, II, 5, Vol. 17, Kassel: Bärenreiter, 2003.

3.
IL MIO TESORO

The picture of conflict in the character of Don Ottavio, defined up to this point primarily through an analysis of the libretto and an examination of the history of the tenor voice, is perfectly complemented by the findings of the following musical analysis of 'Il mio tesoro', the aria originally written for Vienna. 'Il mio tesoro' shows how Don Ottavio's chivalrous grace stands in contrast to the role of avenger that is demanded of him.[52]

Shirley Trembath tried to use the form of 'Il mio tesoro' (and 'Dalla sua pace') to draw conclusions about the character of Don Ottavio: 'The circularity and conservativeness of the da capo arias of Don Ottavio are fundamental to Mozart's portrayal of Don Ottavio as a man incapable of action. [...] A connection can be made between Ottavio's weak character and the ternary design of his two arias.'[53] Trembath sees both 'Il mio tesoro' (and 'Dalla sua pace') in the tradition of the Baroque da capo aria: 'Don Ottavio's two arias resemble the da capo aria of Baroque opera because they follow the standard pattern – ABA – each section being about the same length, the second section representing a clear contrast to the A sections.'[54] But the da capo aria is 'undramatic because it is circular; it turns back on itself instead of projecting into the future.'[55] This is precisely why the da capo aria was increasingly replaced by 'binary types'[56] with the tendency toward the plot-driven dynamic aria in the late 18th century.

In her argumentation, Trembath recognizes the danger of oversimplifying the link between form and character. She must acknowledge that even dynamic characters sometimes sing arias

52. The real problem for a coherent portrait of the figure of Don Ottavio turns out to be 'Dalla sua pace', the aria composed subsequently for the Vienna premiere. Cf. Rohringer, 'Don Ottavio: Figur versus Medium. Zum Verhältnis von Prager und Wiener Fassung des *Don Giovanni*,' *Musik & Ästhetik* 58, pp. 5–32.
53. Trembath 1993, p. 990.
54. Trembath 1993, p. 987.
55. Ibid.
56. Ibid.

of the 'ternary type,'[57] so to maintain her basic idea, she endeavors to explain away such instances as exceptions. Even Don Giovanni's aria 'Meta di voi qua vadano' is a 'type of ternary but could hardly be regarded as a "standard" ternary'[58], contends Trembath, and Figaro's 'Se vuol ballare' is, after all, a parody: 'in this aria the conservatism is not the singer's but the object of Figaro's derision, Count Almaviva.'[59]

In 'Il mio tesoro' we can observe a clear return to the formal principles of the sonata and concerto.[60] This mixing of forms is not a deviation that can be restricted to the pre-Classical or early Classical period, but a phenomenon in evidence throughout the 18th century.[61] That is precisely why this type of return in 'Il mio tesoro', taken on its own, does not yet contradict Trembath's proposition that this is a da capo aria. One can express doubts about this assessment, however.

The linking of sonata form and da capo aria means that the A section acts as the sonata's main subject while the B section comprises the modulating transition and cadence in the secondary key. An additional thematic contrast in the form of a secondary subject is typically dispensed with – a method that is, of course, also familiar from instrumental music. The same applies to the lack of a distinct development.[62] This function can be restricted to a retransition to the original key. The da capo of A that follows could be seen from the perspective of the sonata form as

---

57. Ibid.
58. Ibid.
59. Ibid., 993.
60. Structural principles of instrumental and concert music are also found on the 'surface' through the tendency toward long high notes and the use of coloratura in connection with cadential points and return transitions.
61. Cf. Christian Möllers 'Der Einfluß des Konzertsatzes auf die Formentwicklung im 18. Jahrhundert,' *Zeitschrift für Musiktheorie* 9, 1978, pp. 34–46; Charles Rosen *Sonata Forms. Revised Edition,* New York & London: Norton, 1988; and Markus Neuwirth, 'Does a "monothematic" expositional design have tautological implications for the recapitulation? An alternative approach to "altered recapitulations" in Haydn,' *Studia Musicologica*, (publication pending).
62. James Hepokowski and Warren Darcy, *Elements of Sonata Theory. Norms, Types, and Deformations in the Late-Eighteenth-Century Sonata*, Oxford: Oxford University Press, 2006, refer to a 'Type 1 Sonata' (especially pp. 343–352).

an abbreviated recapitulation in which only the main subject is repeated. This last point, in particular, illustrates that although principles familiar from the sonata form are used, this nevertheless remains primarily a da capo form. An extension of the cadential portion of A' does not alter the fundamental ternary nature of the form. A paradigmatic example of this type is 'Un'aura amorosa', Ferrando's first aria in 'Così fan tutte'. A comprises bars 1–23, B bars 23–41 and A' bars 42–73 or 42–80 if one includes the final orchestral ritornello.

But that which follows the da capo of the A section in 'Il mio tesoro' (bars 87 ff.) is not simply an outward extension of A' but a recomposition of B. To correspond to the changed tonal relationships in the da capo, the *Quintabsatz* (Heinrich Christophe Koch) in the secondary key (bars 29–35) must be replaced by that in the primary key – a process that once again suggests the sonata principle. In 'Il mio tesoro', this substitution occurs in conjunction with a restructuring of the motivic-thematic surface whose central manifestation is now derived from bar 39. The functional equivalence of B and B' is underscored by the retention of the textual correlation. Finally, coming as the second section of B' starting in bar 79 is the initially transposed and then greatly extended cadential section, already familiar from the exposition (bars 36 ff.).

It is therefore appropriate to question whether 'Il mio tesoro' in its primary form is a da capo aria. Such an interpretation would have to regard bars 1–29 as the A section, bars 29–49 as the B section and bars 49–101 as a disproportionately extended A' whose scope is equal to that of A and B combined. Given the structural principles of the sonata form, a more convincing interpretation is a large binary division in which B (or B') is further subdivided: A (bars 8–29), B_1 (29–35) and B_2 (36–48) is followed by the second part with the repetition of A (49–70) and the recomposition of B with B_1' (70–78) and B_2' (79–93).

This formal concept is enclosed by opening and closing orchestral ritornelli, establishing a further link to the concerto form, though this connection only exists in the outward formal framework. Since B is followed not by a separate middle episode C but a direct return to A', there is no need for an introductory middle ritornello to C. From the perspective of the sonata form, this means that 'Il mio tesoro' is also lacking a distinct development section. Instead, there is an elaborate soloistic return transition in the form of coloratura (bars 43–48) – an entrance of the type familiar from instrumental rondo forms.

The form of 'Il mio tesoro' accommodates the binary nature of the text by portraying not just a mere contrast but, in the nature of a 'action aria'[63], an inner development: After Don Ottavio in the A section asks those present to console Donna Anna, the transformation to a vengeance aria is completed in the B section with his announced desire to return only as the messenger of the bloody deed. The sonata principle is able to open up the form tonally and enable momentum at the motivic-thematic level to support the libretto. After the recapitulation of A, of course, it is not until the recomposition of B, where it is only the substitution of the section formulas that allows the sonata form-specific aspect of the overall tonal structure to emerge clearly, that we have a peripeteia and the final breakthrough from *caritas* to *vendetta* succeeds.[64]

Nevertheless, Don Ottavio's determination in 'Il mio tesoro' seems relativized, not because of the mere repetition of A as Trembath mistakenly holds, but rather because of the form of the closing ritornello. The orchestral postlude initially promises a brief affirmation of the heroic gesture that ends Don Ottavio's vocal part (bars 93 f.) but is then surprisingly interrupted by a short lament (bar 95), after which the music returns to the *grazioso* nature of the opening, which is the true final sentiment.

The thematic manifestation used here derives from bars 19/20, whose introduction there is of special note because it is the first passage where the upper voice of the orchestra is not *colla*

63. The term commonly used for this in German scholarship is *Aktionsarie* (Kunze 1984, 288).

64. In *Le nozze di Figaro,* the Count's aria 'Vedrò mentre io sospiro' represents the genre of vengeance aria. It is a binary type, consisting of *Allegro maestoso* and *Allegro assai*. Nowhere does the ascending structure of this aria suggest a da capo: the Count's momentum is unbroken. By comparison, the sequence of 'return' (bars 49 ff.) – 'breakthrough' (bars 70 ff.) make the character of Don Ottavio in 'Il mio tesoro' seem entirely idiosyncratic.

parte with the vocal part – even though the vocal part in bar 19 initially only echoes the melody of bar 16. Considering that the counterpoint to the long note in the vocal part (bar 24 f.) appears to be the proper place to introduce a new motif, the functional differentiation of the thematic structure in bars 19/20 seems strangely premature.

The bar preceding bars 19/20 is in turn bar 3 from the opening ritornello. The length of the rhythmic value there and at the beginning of bar 4 makes it easier to see the second half of the bar, with its subdivision into quarter notes, in terms of the *alla breve* meter as well. This effect is supported by the structural diastematics falling by a half step from E-flat to D within each bar. In bars 19 and 20, on the other hand, we observe in the foreground an upward jump to the second half of each bar. The accompanying melodic emphasis contradicts the previous and regular metrics in *alla breve*, in which customarily the second half is lighter than the first. Since each of the two bars only leads to the composing-out of the same structural note in the middleground – first D and then E-flat, both part of the ascent to the fifth at F – the metric impulse in the second half of each bar remains without any proper function. The repeated emphasis of the structural note in the middleground seems redundant.

Figure 1. Il mio tesoro, bars 15–23, structural outline

Starting with the opening ritornello, Mozart combined two 'open' two-bar phrases with a cadential three-bar phrase. This pattern remained intact for the first vocal phrase, though a different cadential formula was substituted. In the consequent, this pattern is initially extended to 2+2+4 bars, and in the final closing, the four-bar phrase is lengthened to six bars. In this context, further subdividing the individual bars 19 and 20 inhibits the construction of a higher-level two-bar phrase. This counterpoint works against Don Ottavio's dramatic emphasis.

Figure 2. Il mio tesoro, conclusion

A related effect is repeated at the very end of the aria: Don Ottavio finishes his part with a cadential phrase of 2+2+2 bars (bars 88–93). The closing ritornello initially adheres to the two-bar structure (93f.). But the standalone bar 95 – the *lamento* – breaks this pattern. Although the music promptly returns to the previous pattern with the concluding phrase of 2+4 bars, the reappearance of the *grazioso* motif lends it an inherent 'metric-rhythmic ritardando' that blunts the heroism of Don Ottavio.[65] Only in the very last bars does the orchestra return to the dynamic habitus.[66]

Even Trembath comments on this point and interprets it in the context of her overall analysis: 'Once again, Don Ottavio turns back.'[67] The question, however, is who exactly 'turns back' here. The fact that the motivic material derives solely from the orchestral counterpoint and does not enter into Don Ottavio's melodic material suggests a distinction between the explicit narrative of Don Ottavio (text) and the implicit narrative of Mozart's orchestra (subtext). One could therefore speak of a 'coded message' sent from the 'omniscient' author, Mozart, to the audience. Don Ottavio is carried away by the feeling of his own power, and one might therefore suspect that the 'initiation rite' portrayed earlier was a success, but the orchestra's commentary is followed closely by the denial.

Ultimately, this makes 'Il mio tesoro' a musical symbol for the impossible unity of the hero and lover in the tenor role in the closing years of the 18th century. We recognize what Don Ottavio is unable to recognize, perhaps even in the *scena ultima* of *Don Giovanni*. In the era of the conquering baritones, even with the castrato absent from the stage, the tenor still comes up short in the affairs of the heart.

---

65. This contradicts the view of Stefan Kunze (1984) that 'the basis of the large, representative gesture of 'Il mio tesoro' lies in the unique combination of *andante grazioso* and broad *alla breve* movement [In der eigenartigen Kombination von andante grazioso und und weiträumiger Alla-breve-Bewegung liegt der Ansatzpunkt für die große, repräsentative Geste]' (p. 425). The representative gesture does not stem from the combination at all but from the broad *alla breve* alone.

66. 'Il mio tesoro', with its interruption of the dynamic impulse through the orchestral coda, resembles Donna Anna's 'Or sai chi l'onore', where the orchestra retreats conspicuously to a low-register *piano* for the conclusion. This construction would offer a basis for similar conclusions regarding the character of Donna Anna. The gesture in 'Or sai chi l'onore', unlike that in 'Il mio tesoro', does not of course refer to a contrasting or earlier affect that seems to retract the current sentiment. Instead, the suddenness of this type of 'slamming on of the brakes' stands for the character's utter breakdown. This anticipates the third aria of Donna Anna, 'Non mi dir, bell'idol mio', with its primarily distanced tone despite the presence of some coloratura (bars 83 ff.).

67. Trembath 1993, p. 990.

DON GIOVANNI THEN AND NOW: TEXT AND PERFORMANCE

Sergio Durante

When approaching a work like Da Ponte and Mozart's *Don Giovanni*, a person with any degree of historical consciousness feels a special responsibility. After all, this work has been defined as the 'opera of all operas' (E.T.A. Hoffmann) and, while such an evaluation represents an exaggeration, it is still a widely circulating one. We therefore approach the work with the respect due to the great masterpieces of world-literature, as we would works by Shakespeare or Dante. This attitude is perhaps a mistake – at least insofar as the quoted authors, had they a word on the matter, would probably endorse a passionate and direct appreciation rather than a cold, distant one. And yet, as a consequence of our Western frame of mind, we cannot lightly dismiss the problem of understanding a work of art through the powerful lens of history.

The focus of this essay is on performance, that is, on those problems connected with the re-enactment of a piece of musical theatre. This approach, it must be confessed, does not make a significant difference with respect to a 'purely' intellectual discourse on the opera, in that 'performance' must be understood here in a broad sense. Were we solely concerned with practical aspects of production, we should admit to be working with the wrong tools: it is idle to speak about practical problems without referring specifically to a theatre (its stage, size and technical facilities), a cast, an orchestra, a budget allowing us to foresee how much a production will invest in stage sets, costumes, and rehearsals. Therefore, the performance orientation we might usefully ruminate upon is concerned with underlying cultural structures, above which one might then start to do things such as administer a budget, conduct an orchestra, direct a cast, design a set and use a theatrical space.

I will discuss, in particular, two intertwined planes: in the first, selected aspects of the opera will be touched upon from the standpoint of reception, in order to introduce and/or clarify, to some extent, the controversial theme of the opera's meaning and of its historical identity. In the second, I will turn to structural analysis (both verbal and musical), as the language of scholarly literature, and attempt to disclose some implications for the understanding of the work. Whilst I have no pretensions to completeness, the different 'types' of discourse on *Don Giovanni* offer a palette of methodological tools that the reader may find useful for his own decision-making on performance.

PART I
RECEPTION

Concerning the 'then' and 'now' of the title, it should be clear that these are almost symbolic terms, in that, especially in the case of *Don Giovanni*, with its two authorial versions of Prague 1787 and Vienna 1788, there is not a single 'then'. Nor is there is a single 'now', since the productions of this work throughout history offer a very broad range of different 'renderings'. I share the view that the process of transmission and reception of a work of art is dynamic and indefinitely mobile, and that the identity itself of a work of art is constantly in play. And yet, within the rich, complicated and not entirely investigated reception history of *Don Giovanni,* I will distinguish two main and relatively identifiable traditions, the first one – relative to the original *Don Giovanni* – is faithful (in intention at least) to the musico-dramatic text as defined by Lorenzo Da Ponte and Wolfgang Mozart; the second one, that we shall name the 'romantic' *Don Giovanni*, is mainly based on the interpretation of E.T.A. Hoffmann and offers a radically different image of the title-role and of the entire set of relations established between the characters.

In the last analysis, the first Don Giovanni (as a character) is plainly a cynical rascal; he might and does attract the sympathy of the spectator, but the main point of the plot is to exhibit the progress of his recklessness, leading to the final and fully-deserved punishment. Giovanni is in some sense a hero but, if so, he reveals himself as such only in his final refusal to deny his self, to repent and change his life. Within this general characterization, the opera is a relatively simple story of crime and punishment set within a well-established theatrical genre, opera buffa, the conventions of which are relevant for a sound understanding of the subject. It may well be that such traditions were taken forward by both librettist and composer towards unusually original elaborations, but they should not be ignored. There is no doubt, for instance, that the stock 'noble couple' of the genre is portrayed here by Donna Anna and Don Ottavio and that both characters share a common general characterization. This suggests a straightforward interpretation of the opera within the reception conditions of both Prague and Vienna, a theatrical venue that, in Mary Hunter's words, privileged the quest for 'sheer pleasure'.[1]

This was possibly too simple for an intellectually aristocratic audience. And in fact the purpose of Hoffmann in his *Phantasiestück* of 1813 was to transcend the understanding of commoners when he commented that 'nobody [has] yet foreseen the more profound meaning of this opera of all operas'[2].

I am conscious that a dual representation of the multifaceted *Don Giovanni* tradition is a simplification of historical reality, but I also sense that it holds true – at least insofar as the perception of the public of the early 21st century goes; therefore, I shall try to build a line of thought upon this provisional dichotomy.[3]

This first tradition is characteristic of the very beginning of the work's performance history and never disappeared entirely during

---

1. M. Hunter, *The Culture of opera buffa in Mozart's Vienna*, Princeton: Princeton, University Press, 1999.

2. '[…] wohl keiner die tiefere Bedeutung der Oper aller Opern auch nur ahnete' in E.T.A. Hoffmann, *Don Juan. Eine fabelhafte Begebenheit, die sich mit einem reisenden Enthusiasten zugetragen*, first published in the *Allgemeine musikalische Zeitung* of Leipzig in 1813 and quoted here from E.T.A. Hoffmann, *Fantasiestücke in Callot's Manier. Werke 1814*, H. Steinecke ed. in collaboration with G. Allroggen and W. Segebrecht, Frankfurt am Main: Deutscher Klassiker Verlag, 1993, p. 90 .

3. Among the recent valuable works on the transmission and reception of *Don Giovanni* in France, Italy and England, see S. Arienta, *Don Giovanni. Le manipolazioni di un testo nell'Europa della Restaurazione*, Milano: Ricordi, 1994; this work is however less concerned with the reception of the opera in the German speaking world, to which my attention will be especially directed.

the following decades. At that time, the opera would be performed in German in one of various extant translations, the most important of which was the one published by Friedrich Rochlitz in 1801 and appended to the Breitkopf & Härtel edition of the score.[4] It should be pointed out that the early German translations departed from Da Ponte in significant details, without necessarily distorting the image of the main character. For instance the version by Johann Gottlieb Neefe for the Mannheim production of September 1789 changed the name of Don Ottavio to 'Herr Fischblut', an eloquent indication that the nature of this character had undergone alteration well before Hoffmann.[5] To what extent the change was received and internalized by audiences is impossible to say but evidently the 'noble pair' of the *opera buffa* was no longer (or, at least, not necessarily) a relevant entity. In any case, the translation into German meant that genre being referenced was no longer that of *opera buffa* but *Singspiel*, with spoken dialogues performed by German actors/singers for their native audiences.

If the alteration of Don Ottavio's character dates back to 1789, it is only with Hoffmann's interpretation that the 'demonic' element so dear to the romantic spirit is fully developed to the extent of reshaping the plot. He envisioned the relationship between Don Giovanni and Donna Anna 'through music alone and without consideration of the literary text'.[6] Hoffmann would hardly believe how influential his fictional tale was for the later understanding of this opera and yet, for all that his interpretation was so successful and long-lasting, it is difficult to accept that this influence was the individual consequence of an intervention by one uniquely shameless visionary. In the

4. *Don Juan. Oper in zwei Akten. Nach dem Italienischen des Abb. Da Ponte frei bearbeitet von Friedrich Rochlitz*, Leipzig, Breitkopf & Härtel 1801. A recent comparative study of this translation is found in V. Confuorto, *Il Don Juan di Friedrich Rochlitz (Lipsia 1801) e la germanizzazione dell'opera di Da Ponte-Mozart*, unpublished diss., University of Padua: a.y., 2007/08.

5. Noteworthy in the Rochlitz is the omission of lines which portrayed the manly commitment of Ottavio (such as – in Da Ponte – I, 3: 'tutto il mio sangue / verserò se bisogna / ma dov'è il scellerato?').

6. "[...] in der Musik, ohne alle Rücksicht auf den Text das ganze Verhältnis der beiden [...] erschein" (op. cit., p. 95).

romantic *Don Juan* the title role is (secretly) beloved by Donna Anna, rather than her would-be rapist – and in fact there has been no proper rape because:

> The fire of a superhuman sensuality, glowing from Hell, flowed through her innermost being and made her impotent to resist. Only he, only Don Giovanni, could arouse in her the lustful abandon with which she embraced him […][7]

This constitutes a major change and one that implies also a side-characterization of Don Ottavio who turns from affectionate lover and noble defender of Anna's honour into a mediocre fop: 'cold, common, effeminate'.[8] If 'Herr Fischblut' was the precedent, Hoffmann fully developed the consequences.

But this is not the only hint that Hoffmann's reading was 'prepared' – so to speak – by details of the German translations circulating at the time. Already, in the first translation by Neefe, which is altogether close to Da Ponte, some new key-words seem to moderate the profile of Don Giovanni, or rather to justify his conduct on the basis of a code of honour. For instance, while in Da Ponte he is addressed by the Commendatore before the duel as 'vile' (on account of the violence he inflicts on a woman), Neefe has 'Verwegener' (reckless) and immediately afterwards a climaxing 'Feiger' (coward) which sounds like a provocation. 'Feiger' is further emphasized in the 'frei bearbeitet' version of Friedrich Rochlitz, where Don Juan reacts patently as the offended one:

Governor:	Feiger, Verbrecher -
Don Juan:	Feiger? Ich?
Governor:	Feiger!
Don Juan:	Zittre! Bald soll dir dein Trotz vergehn![9]

7. 'Das Feuer eine übermenschlichen Sinnlichkeit, Glut aus der Hölle durchströmte ihr Innerstens und machte jeden Widerstand vergeblich. Nur Er, nur Don Juan, konnte der wohllüstigen Wahnsinn in ihr entzünden, mit dem sie ihn umfing […]' (op. cit., p. 95), translation by B. Williams, *Don Juan as an Idea*, in *The Don Giovanni moment. Essays on the Legacy of an Opera*, L. Goehr and D. Herwitz eds., New York: Columbia University Press, 2006, pp. 107-117, p. 110.
8. "[…] kalten, unmännlichen, ordinären" (*Ibid.*).
9. Commendatore: Coward, criminal / Don Juan: Coward? Me? / Commendatore: Coward! / Don Juan: Tremble, you will soon regret your arrogance.

It has been suggested that Hoffmann's tale was written in reaction to the version by Rochlitz, whose moralizing attitude it reverses. I do not deny this; as far as the general characterization of the plot is concerned, the thesis, advanced by Ricarda Schmidt, is reasonable.[10] It is significant, however, that seeds of the heroic Don Giovanni can be traced back to the beginning of its diffusion in Germany.

The detail concerning Don Ottavio is tiny but revealing. More important for the modernization of the subject are certain longer *tirades* by Rochlitz, such as the circuitous seduction of Zerlina, which appears a pretext for presenting a bourgeois criticism of the aristocracy analogous to the disdain for the lower social class revealed in the 'new' cemetery scene. The latter significantly omits Don Giovanni's narration of his adventure with Leporello's girlfriend. In Da Ponte, this episode occurs right before the manifestation of the Commendatore's ghost and clearly prepares that dramatic climax. Therefore, a significant stage of Don Giovanni's progress – the climaxing betrayal of his only supporter – is omitted.

In Rochlitz, the finale of Act I is transformed into a *locus classicus* of romantic sensibility, turning a metaphor by Da Ponte ('My head is confused / I do not know what I am doing / and a horrible storm / my God, threatens me'[11]) into a thunderstorm scene which remained in the performing tradition for a long time. The 'suspension' of the action at the end of Act I, characteristic of opera buffa, appears to have been felt as a problem for the modern public. In fact, Hoffmann himself, who claims to be attending a performance in the Italian original, in reality reports a duel scene, which significantly distorts the original. But we shall come back to this at a later point.

Don Giovanni's drive towards women, his acquisitive anxiety, is replaced in Hoffmann by a search for perfection. Already, before Hoffmann, however, Rochlitz had omitted the line by Da Ponte that precludes such idealistic interpretation: 'He conquers

10. R. Schmidt, *Wenn mehrere Künste im Spiel sind. Intermedialität bei E.T.A. Hoffmann*, Göttingen: Vandenhoeck & Ruprecht, 2006.

11. 'E' confusa la mia testa / non so più quello ch'io mi faccia / e un'orribile tempesta minacciando / oddio mi va.'

old ladies / for the sake of adding to the list'.[12]) Juan becomes, for Hoffmann, the representation of the innermost spirit of life as iconicized in carnal pleasure and his conduct is justified as the outcome of an irresistible desire for absolute liberty. He is the epitome of freedom, with clear Faustian resonances, devoid of social obligations and moral constraints.

It is clear that the *Don Juan* by Hoffmann (for which a new *Zeitgeist* had already paved the way) represents a strong twist of the Da Ponte-Mozart version.[13] However, long before the most recent literature scholarly literature stressed this problem, *Don Juan* had been severely rejected as fancy in Otto Jahn's seminal biography of 1856-59. Kicked out of the door, however, he kept coming back in through the window. For instance, when Hermann Abert revised Jahn's book in his biography of 1919-1921, he refuted some points of the anti-romantic approach of his predecessor. The original *buffo* element, residing in the recurrent erotic failures of Don Giovanni, was re-interpreted thus:

> [...] it is hardly, as Jahn would want us to believe, the cause of the "gaiety which permeates the whole opera". It should rather be regarded as a very effective element in the characterization of a hero. A character such as his has to be strengthened by continual opposition; his energy is kept in a state of constant tension, driving him to his fate. Besides, the main point of Don Giovanni's nature is not his ability to seduce this or that woman who happens to cross his path, even if there were 'a thousand and three', but the elemental, sensual urge to live and love which he has uncontrolled energy to satisfy. The more he reveals himself, the more dangerous, but also the greater, he becomes.

Not only the 'Hoffmannesque' interpretation, artistic in intention, but also the scholarly one by Abert, goes awry under the spell of an established paradigm.

---

12. Leporello (catalogue aria) 'Delle vecchie fa conquista / pel piacer di porle in lista'.) Rochlitz replaced it with generic remarks on cynicism.
13. For an outline on this matter see J. Rushton, *W. A. Mozart. Don Giovanni*, Cambridge: C.U.P., 1981.

* * *

Deviations from a text, of course, occur all the more easily when translation is involved, but that is not the only communication medium. As we shall see, the very same musico-dramatic text might be realised or understood in different ways in performance, with or without the aid of the literary precedents circulating in European literature (from Tirso de Molina to Molière and Goldoni) on account of the semantic ambiguity of music. No doubt Mozart's score adds an expressive depth beyond the words of Da Ponte – even against them, in rare cases such as 'Batti batti bel Masetto' – but because of music's inherent ambiguity, it does not have the capacity on its own to build a substantially different story or constellation of characters. Where the level of ambiguity is high our interpretation should be prudent; on the other hand, controversial issues may be overcome (or else exploited as interpretive tools) through their reduction to apodictic statements. For instance, Andrew Steptoe on Elvira:[14]

> The enigmatic Elvira occupies the ambivalent middle ground in temperament [i.e. between seria and buffa characterization], just as she does in purely musical terms. But when she adopts the graver tones of Anna and Ottavio, the ironic intention is again clear[15] as in the aria "Ah fuggi il traditor". Here is a woman who has already succumbed to temptation [...] denying the same pleasure to another, and she does so with formal archaic severity. The words show an exaggerated, histrionic hostility, quite inappropriate for the simple task of cautioning a peasant maid.

But is the 'ironic intention' of the aria obvious beyond any doubt? Stephan Kunze, in a passage on the same musical number, presents a different opinion, pointing instead to the 'noble and

14. A. Steptoe, *The Mozart-Da Ponte Operas. The Cultural and Musical Background to* Le nozze di Figaro, Don Giovanni, *and* Così fan tutte, Oxford: Clarendon Press, 1988, p. 201.

15. One must point out that when Steptoe evokes irony, he is referring to a supposed ironic intention of the composer, the recipient of which is the spectator (not to irony played among the characters on stage). Irony is a rhetorical figure often implied or actually prescribed by Da Ponte (e.g. in Act I, sc. 20 'Masetto dirà questo verso in tono ironico'), but that is a different communication level.

archaic deportment'[16] of Elvira, one which will be immediately grasped by Ottavio and Anna later in the Quartet 'Non ti fidar, o misera'. Rather than focussing on the communicative function ('the simple task of cautioning a peasant maid'), Kunze digs into the expressive potential:[17]

> The opposing forces of desperate agitation and of restraint produce a barely tolerable tension. What will the effect be on the already dominated Zerlina of this epic, mythic-archaic exit of the noble figure of Elvira, marked as it is by an infinite grief? It is the clash of two worlds.

Who is right? My preference is for Kunze but let me suggest that Steptoe's reading is possible (albeit wrong with respect to the text as a whole), or rather 'performable': the twist from serious to ironic is in the hands (and body) of the actress/singer (or whoever instructs her towards such effect). More precisely, Steptoe's reading is performable within the momentary situation of Act I, sc. 10 in that the 'twist' does not contradict the verbal text and the music is flexible or ambiguous enough to allow for it. However, the contradiction is clear with respect to other points in the plot (namely sc. 5 and 6, the aforementioned Quartet and the 'masked' Terzetto where the musical characterization is particularly unambiguous). The hoax of Act II, when Don Giovanni cheats Elvira again, only to leave her deceived with Leporello in disguise, is pure 'theatre of cruelty', one of the many variations on the theme of Don Giovanni's cynicism. It could be cited as a proof of Elvira weakness or foolishness (*la pazza*, is she named by Leporello) but not, retrospectively, of a rhetorical exaggeration in the earlier 'Ah fuggi il traditor'. And her later behaviour in the opera strengthens her nobility, both as would-be saver of Don Giovanni's soul and in her final choice of atonement and renunciation of the mundane world.

* * *

16. S. Kunze, *Il teatro di Mozart. Dalla Finta semplice al Flauto magico*, Venezia: Marsilio, 1990, p.512.
17. S. Kunze, op.cit., p. 513.

The reverberations of the Don Giovanni character, in literature and in the realm of the newly-founded discipline 'history of opera', during the 19th Century are numerous and culturally relevant. Two recent publications contribute fresh investigations on this theme, making it clear among other things that Mozart's *Don Giovanni* and the literary or philosophical one are two different entities. I refer to *The Don Giovanni Moment. Essays on the Legacy of an Opera* (2007) and especially to *Mozarts Oper als literarisches Ereignis: E.T.A. Hoffmann Don Juan-Novelle und ihre Folgen* within the *Mozarts Opern Handbuch* (2007). If, then, a degree of order in the understanding of this opera is restored (or is under restoration), the long-lasting effects of the heroic image are still with us. It is not surprising that Pierre Jean Jouve took for granted the seduction of Donna Anna in a book published in 1941 and in the revised edition in 1968 (though it is perhaps more surprising that the book is still reprinted):[18]

> Donna Anna, ruffled hair, pursues out of her house a disguised man. She wants to reach him, she wants at the same time to chase, to protect and to punish him; most of all she wants to see the masked face, she wants to know who is the seducer who abused her.

As late as the second centennial of *Don Giovanni* in 1987 Ludwig Finscher stated:[19]

> The history of the work is the extreme case of a reception history, that became estranged almost entirely from the work itself, from what is

18. «Donna Anna échevelée poursuit hors de sa maison un visiteur voilé. Elle veut l'atteindre; elle veut tout à la fois le chasser, le garder et le punir ; surtout elle veut connaître le visage masqueé, elle veut savoir qui est le séducteur, qui a abusé d'elle» in Pierre Jean Jouve, *Le Don Juan de Mozart*, Paris, Christian Bourgois 1968 (first published 1941), p. 43.
19. „Die Geschichte des Werkes ist der Extremfall einer Rezepzionsgeschichte, die sich fast gänzlich vom Werk selbst, von dem, was im Text und in der Partitur dargestellt und gemeint ist, entfernt hat; einer Rezepzionsgeschichte [...], die uns weniger über das Werk sagt als über seine Rezipienten" in L. Finscher, *Don Giovanni 1987*, in *Mozart-Jahrbuch 1987/88*, pp. 19-27, p. 27.

> represented and meant by the text and the score; a reception history [...] which tells us less about the work than about its recipients.

And most recently, the quest for a faithful approach to *Don Giovanni* has been reflected in the title of a book chapter by Dieter Borchmeyer: *Um eine Don Giovanni ohne 19. Jahrhundert bittend* (For a *Don Giovanni* without 19th Century).[20]

These characterizations call for comment. The romantic interpretation of *Don Giovanni* was certainly not the only one to reach the stage during the 19th and 20th centuries; it would be interesting to ascertain how many of the productions conformed to the 'romantic' mould, how many were more or less faithful to the original, and finally, how many followed yet other – under investigated and less influential – courses. Such a study was undertaken by Ch. Bitter in his *Wandlungen in den Inszenierungsformen des 'Don Giovanni'* of 1961,[21] a rich if not always satisfactory study by current scholarly standards. Even if Bitter's investigation had been more accurate and complete, and had it considered in detail the fifty-odd translations and/or adaptations of this work, it still could not have entirely explained the success of the tradition of a romantic *Don Juan*, simply because this is based on a rather inextricable combination of theatrical, literary and philosophical factors. Whatever the outcome of statistics, the prevailing concept applied to *Don Giovanni* has been for decades (and still is in certain quarters) the 'romantic' one, much to the impatience of learned music-historians. Evidently this image is not only perpetuated by individual theatrical productions, but also represents a cultural tradition, of which the theatrical one is but a part.

It is puzzling that an interpretation that is declaredly fantastical in nature and confuted by authoritative critics and historians should have such long-lasting effects. Why this should be so, and how it became possible, is a matter for reflection. Was it the merit of a German writer fashionable in his time, the intuition of a genius, an oversight of academia or a collective illusion? As

20. Dieter Borchmeyer, *Mozart oder Die Entdeckung der Liebe*, Frankfurt a.M. – Leipzig: Insel, 2005, p. 142.
21. Regensburg: Bosse, 1961.

I have tried to demonstrate, if Hoffmann represents the catalyst, his success is probably the result of a combination of processes.

* * *

Of course, a romantic Don Juan was vital for the survival of the opera in the age of Romanticism. The focus on one character is typical in this sense, as opposed to the rationalistic geometries of the couples; also 'romantic' in character is the sympathy for those aspects, originally meant as *buffi*, soon re-interpreted in the ennobled key of romantic irony. Such a re-interpretation appears to inform, for instance, the new relationship between Don Juan and Leporello in the version by Rochlitz.[22] 'Romantic', too, is the elevation of the title-role to a transcendental dimension, so that the relevant philosophical elements are beyond the verbal text and in the realm of hermeneutics – where commentators may discuss, for instance, the 'real' feelings of Donna Anna towards Don Giovanni, invoking a reality beyond her actual words. From a critical perspective, this is a crucial point in the history of reception in that, beyond it, it becomes futile to refute on a philological basis aspects of hyper-interpretation – all the more so because such exercises are, generally speaking, in good intellectual standing and tend to be self-generating. Like it or not, this has been the destiny of *Don Giovanni*. It goes against the grain of a historico-philological sensibility; but the question is whether we should moralistically choose between one approach or the other, or accept them both as legitimate offspring of European culture.

An important step towards acceptance is realizing that some elements of Hoffmann's interpretation were 'in the air', not in an abstract sense, but in concrete factors such as the obliteration of the *opera buffa* conventions within the performing traditions of the German stage; the consequent transformation of pivotal characters like Don Giovanni and Don Ottavio; and, more importantly, the modern notion that music is a language

22. I refer in particular to the long original dialogue added in Act I, sc. 4 in which the arguments of traditional morals (Leporello) and those of Juan are juxtaposed; equally important in this new scene are the indications of the para-text which delineate a new style of stage presentation.

independent of words but thereby superior to verbal language in its capacity to communicate. Only upon such a theoretical basis, presented by Friedrich Wilhelm Wackenroder only a few years after Mozart's death and developed by Hoffmann himself in his writings on instrumental music, was it possible to build the new *Don Giovanni*. That premise justified, and even called for, unconstrained alterations of the verbal text. Rochlitz explained in the *Vorerinnerung* to his *Frei Bearbeitung* that:[23]

> I am solely responsible for the choice to maintain a distance sometimes not only from the words but also the meaning of the Italian text. I did that because convinced that it was better to elicit the text from the wonderful music and not from the rhymes, sometimes muddled, of the Libretto.

That this was not an isolated episode, but a pervasive cultural attitude through the 19th century and later, is proven by the complicated history of the German translations of *Don Giovanni*, yet to be written in full but outlined already in 1887 by Rudolf von Freisauff.[24] It is the fascinating and paradoxical story of the quest for one definitive, 'authentic *Don Juan* text' worthy to become the standard in German theatres, replacing the many translations in circulation. The project was entrusted in 1883 to a Commission chaired by Baron Perfall, *Intendant* of the Munich Hof- und Nationaltheater, but it quickly came to nothing. Despite the predictable failure, the project and its context tells us a lot about the cultural relevance of the 'Germanization' of *Don Giovanni*. According to Freisauff, the most popular translation in his time was still the one by Rochlitz, for the

23. 'Allem zu tragen habe ich aber, dass ich zuweilen von dem Italiener ganz – nicht nur in den Worten, sondern auch in Sinn – abgegangen bin. Es geschahe in die Űberzeugung, es sei besser gethan, den Text aus den herrlichen Musik, als aus den zuweilen doch etwas ungereimten Reimen des Gedichts zu ziehen.' (Op. cit., p. I).

24. R. von Freisauff, *Mozart's Don Juan 1787-1887, Ein Beitrag zur Geschichte dieser Oper, herausgegeben anlässlich der 100jährigen Jubelfeier der Oper "Don Juan" von der "Internationalen Stiftung Mozarteum in Salzburg"*, Salzburg, Kerber 1887, p. 71.

good reason that it was the one appended to the first Breitkopf & Härtel score of *Don Giovanni*.[25]

A few years after the abortive Perfall commission (vaguely anticipating the 'parallel action' of Robert Musil's *Man Without Qualities*) a new edition of the libretto was published with an introduction by Carl Friedrich Wittmann. This was based once more on the text by Rochlitz (with spoken dialogues) side by side with the text for the recitatives (published by Johann Philipp Samuel Schmidt in 1845). It outlined once more the history of the German translations and yet returned to the popular Rochlitz-Schmidt text rather than claiming to be any kind of utopian 'authentic and definitive' version like the one longed for by Freisauff. An interesting point about this source is that it carries important evidence of theatrical traditions involving the stage action and prescribed by the para-text. These reveal the long-lasting influence of Hoffman. The idea of Donna Anna's infatuation for Don Juan is most clearly 'performed' on stage at the end of Act I, in the scene that Da Ponte had characterized as 'frozen action' and that Hoffmann had imagined (or perhaps seen in the theatre) in the form of a heroic duel in a thunderstorm. And, unsurprisingly, there is also a great deal of evocative action by Anna in the caption reported by Wittman:[26]

---

25. At least until the publication of the so-called *Alte Mozart-Gesamtausgabe* with a translation by Karl Niese in 1872. Even after that, the habits of singers and public alike seem to have granted the survival of the old text, which had become widely known meanwhile. According to Freisauff, 'Am längsten behauptet hat sich seither die Űbersetzung von Rochlitz, welche 1801 erschienen ist; sie verdankt dies trotz ihrer Mangel einzig und allein dem Umstande, dass es bisher ungeachte mancher Versuche noch immer nicht gelungen ist, unter den Directoren der deutschen Bühnen eine Einigung darüber zu erzielen, endlich einen und denselben Text für sämmtliche deutsche Theater zu acceptieren.' (Op. cit., p. 71-72).

26. The edition, undated, must have been published around the last decade of the 19th or the first of the 20th century the translation by Max Kalbeck (first published 1886) is quoted in the introduction (*Don Juan. Oper in zwei Aufzügen von W. A. Mozart. Dichtung von Lorenzo da Ponte (Rochlitz-Schmidt)*, hrsg. von C. F. Wittman, Leipzig, Philipp Reclam jun. (Universal Bibliothek 2646), p. 13. The original scenic caption is as follows: 'Die Vorigen. Don Juan, Leporello, Zerline. Don Juan und Leporello rechts vorn. Don Octavio, Donna Anna, Donna Elvira in der Mitte. Masetto und Zerline links vorn. [...] Juan (benützt die dadurch entstandene Verwirrung, um mit dem entbloßten Degen in der Hand nach der Mitte hin zu entfließen). Leporello (folgt ihm auf den Fersen, ihn mit seinem Körper schützend). Octavio (zieht seinen Degen, um Juan zu verfolgen). Anna (hält ihn zurück).'

> Scene 28 (Don Juan and Leporello on the right forward. Don Octavio, Donna Anna, Donna Elvira in the middle. Masetto and Zerlina left forward) [...]
>
> [End of the finale:]
> The farmers (try to catch Don Juan)
> The servants (hold them back)
> Don Juan (takes advantage of the confusion to escape in the middle with drawn sword)
> Leporello (follows at his heels, protecting him with his body)
> Octavio (draws his sword to pursue Don Juan)
> Anna (holds him back)

It is possible that the perpetuation of this reading has to do with the persistence of certain concomitant cultural conditions: a conception of sexual relations based upon a rigid social code of behaviour (counterbalanced by the unofficial but just as important permissiveness of the brothel); the justification of liberalism (legitimate son of libertinism in the realm of economics) on the basis of special individual gifts; and the success of a transcendental idea of 'love' as the legitimate father of desire and lust (only Anna's love justifies Giovanni). In order to become viable, libertinism had to be transformed into something different, its representation no longer based on social privilege but rather on spiritual superiority, be it an evil one if necessary. One is left to wonder if the decline of Hoffmann's paradigm is related to the downfall of such categories rather than to any scholarly effort.[27]

* * *

Having examined briefly the fortune of *Don Giovanni/Don Juan* from the point of view of its own 'future', let us try to change perspective. It has been observed by Nino Pirrotta among others that the character of Don Giovanni, as circulating in European literature and in *teatro dell'arte* (probably the main vehicle for its

---

27. Also relevant in this context is the rise of feminist reflection, such as the very balanced example in K.A. Brown, *A critical study of the female characters in Mozart's Don Giovanni and Die Zauberflöte*, Ph.D. diss. University of California at Berkeley, 1997.

diffusion), did not originally focus on eroticism *per se*, but rather on the character's inclination towards deception and, most of all, on his atheism.[28] Atheism represents the origin of all other sins, in that God and the final righteous reward or punishment is the only basis of social and spiritual order. The deception of women, then, was but one of Giovanni's misdeeds (albeit one offering a major vehicle for popular entertainment). While it is true that the 18th century and Da Ponte (as well his immediate model, the *Don Giovanni* by Bertati) transfer the main accent onto sexual libertinism, this is strongly oriented towards a quantitative sense (how many women will Don Giovanni add to the list?) and does not correspond to a Romantic transcendental 'eroticism'. On one hand, we are discussing a prerogative of the *ancien régime* aristocracy, on the other, a dream of the 19th century bourgeoisie. If the latter can be considered *Don Giovanni*'s 'future', where did it come from? What was its 'past'?

Let us examine for a moment the hypothesis that Da Ponte's version represents an intermediate state between the 17th Century Don Giovanni – the atheist – and the Romantic Don Juan, in other words a historical 'moment' in which this subject lay in the balance between the old and the new worlds. From this perspective, while the characterization leans clearly towards a new sexual libertinism, the plot carries in its episodic and accumulative structure the fruit of the old seeds. The sins of Don Giovanni are not, in fact, limited to the list of women in Leporello's catalogue, but can also be traced back to the work of literature that inspired Da Ponte, that is, Dante's *Inferno*.[29] There, we find the following:

28. N. Pirrotta, *Don Giovanni in musica. Dall'«Empio punito» a Mozart*, Venezia: Marsilio, 1991, p. 15 ff. For an excellent synthesis on the history of the subject in European literature see H.J. Kreutzer, *Don Juan – From Play to Opera, in Wolfgang Amadeus Mozart. Il dissoluto punito ossia il Don Giovanni. Facsimile of the Autograph Score*, Los Altos Ca.: The Packard Humanities Institute, 2009, pp. 1-11.

29. 'Having found the three subjects [one of which was *Don Giovanni*], I went to the Emperor […] and informed him of my project to write these three works at the same time […] I will write by night for Mozart and I will do as if I were reading Dante's *Inferno*'[(L. Da Ponte, *Memorie*, C. Pagnini ed. Milano Rizzoli, 1960, p. 128 (my translation).

Villainy (Canto III= *e.g.*: Act I,1 and 8 as violence against the weak),
Lust (Canto V = *e.g.:* throughout),
Lavishness (Canto VI = *e.g.*: Act I and II, finale I and II),
Pride (Canto VIII = *e.g.*: Act I, sc. 9),
Violence against God (CantoXIV = *e.g.*: finale II),
Violence against fellow-men (Canto XII = *e.g.*: throughout),
Violence against oneself (Canto XIII = *e.g.:* finale II),
Woman cheating (Canto XVIII = *e.g.*: throughout),
Flattery (Canto XVIII = *e.g.*: Act I, 9, 11, 12),
Hypocrisy (Canto XXIII = *e.g.*: Act I, 12),
Fraudulent advisorship (CantoXXVI = *e.g.*: Act I, 9),
Counterfeiting of persons (Canto XXX = *e.g.*: Act II, sc. I ff.).

These represent an incomplete but abundant list of the Christian sins as analysed by Dante. While the well-known reference in the *Mémoirs* is understood on account of the generic colour of the Overture and second finale, it is possible that more specific memories guided the poet's hand, more or less consciously and directly or through intermediate sources. The libretto can thus be read not only from the point of view of modernity but also from that of its past, as backward-looking and carrying the heritage of an archaic vision of the world, transported within the rationalistic mechanism of *opera buffa.* That Da Ponte's intention might have been conscious is at least doubtful and certainly impossible to prove but this is not of vital importance. It is clear that, one way or another, Dante somehow shaped the librettist's theatrical imagination.[30] From the perspective of the modern theatrical producer, this might point to a change in perspective and to the possibility of considering this piece of world literature not only on account of its progressive potential but also of its archaic subliminal sources.

30. For a recent study on the Classical sources of Da Ponte, see E. Malaspina, *Lorenzo Da Ponte e il latino. In margine alle Memorie,* in *Amicitiae templa serena. Studi in onore di Giuseppe Aricò,* L. Castagna and C. Ribaldi eds., Turin, V&P, 2008, pp. 951-967.

PART II
STRUCTURES

Having examined aspects of historical, philological and aesthetic relevance, I should like to change the point of view, and tackle the body of the work, *Don Giovanni*, as a semantic and formal construction. Research concerned with formal aspects bears a more or less explicitly circular demonstrative purpose. We try to demonstrate how and why a piece of art, usually belonging to the 'canon', is what it is: in other words, a superior piece of art. For most people, this demonstration is not of great importance in that the recognition of a work as 'art' by the social group to which they belong is sufficient. Such is the fascination of beauty, however, that other people cherish the ambition of penetrating into the work and find explanations for it. One way to do so is analysis, or the dissection of the work into its components and the clarification of their mutual relationship. Through this approach we hope to be in a better position to appreciate the details, as well as the work as a whole.

When I refer to 'analysis' I am not thinking specifically about 'musical' analysis, but about the analysis of any component of the work. Given that we are dealing with an opera, we are concerned with structures belonging to different realms (or communication media): words and music in the first place, but also narrative structures of a higher order such as the plot (as defined by the sometimes complicated relation of time, place and epistemic system[31]). The plot is unfolded by the behaviour of the characters (which equals their 'characterization' or, in other words, their coming into being as characters through the things they say and the way in which they are said, largely through the text as consigned to the score, but also through delivery, body language, etc.).

Let us make more concrete this generalization: the segment of musico-dramatic text that is defined by the verbal element (the words) is analyzed in relation to its semantic nature or from the

31. The so-called 'epistemic system' defines what in any 'moment' or 'phase' of the dramatic presentation is 'believed' by a single character or by a group of them.

standpoint of prosody, accentuation, rhymes, etc. The semantic aspect is fundamental and requires a competent reader. To understand a certain meaning appropriately is a basic yet formidable exercise. See, for instance, *Don Giovanni*, Act I, sc.8, line 270:[32]

DON GIOVANNI:
O caro il mio Masetto!
Cara la mia Zerlina! t'esibisco
la mia protezione…[33]

In the word 'protezione', which by itself is just a transitory moment of the exposition, there is an implication which was more readily understood by the contemporary public than by us today. By offering protection, an aristocrat established a personal and mutual relationship with a person of inferior social status: protector and protected were tied by an agreement whereby protection was exchanged for obedience (obedience that in *ancien régime* prevailed over 'territorial' laws). But the kind of protection that Don Giovanni is really offering is disclosed by the following lines:

DON GIOVANNI:
A Leporello che fa dei scherzi all'altre contadine
Leporello…
Cosa fai lì, birbone?
LEPORELLO:
Anch'io, caro padrone,
esibisco la mia protezione.[34]

---

32. Hereon I will refer to the only reliable edition of the libretto, *Il Don Giovanni. Dramma giocoso in due atti. Poesia di Lorenzo Da Ponte. Musica di Mozart*, critical ed. by G. Gronda, Turin: Einaudi, 1995.
33. 'I offer you my protection…'
34. Don Giovanni: *To Leporello who is joking with the other peasant-girls*: What are you doing there, you rascal? – Leporello: I am too, my Lord, offering my protection.

Leporello's patting and touching announces the real meaning of *protezione*, that is, the corrupted version of its meaning as exploited by Don Giovanni. A certain understanding of the historical background is needed in order to appreciate the passage. The example also points out how the performance prescribed by the para-text (in this case joking with, and actually patting or touching the other girls) is indispensable to conveying the meaning. Equally indispensable is the fact that the 'trick' is understood by the public through some sign (in the current performance tradition, one of the peasant-girls screams out): the words alone would not be sufficient and this indicates how verbal and performance structures might be functionally connected. In the above example, there is also a formal detail that is of importance: note how the triple rhyme (birbone / padrone / protezione) defines an articulatory function at the end of this micro-drama. Immediately afterwards, a new action begins (Don Giovanni instructs Leporello on how to distract the party and Masetto, so that he can try to seduce Zerlina). While this is only one of the many puns within the larger dramatic 'motif' in the plot that defines the relationship of master and servant, there are other passages – entrusted to verbal communication alone – that are of capital importance for the understanding of larger structures. In the following case, the passage arguably encapsulates the whole plot:

Act I, sc. 14 (after Anna's exit aria 'Or sai chi l'onore'):
Don Ottavio solo
Come mai creder deggio
di sì nero delitto
capace un cavaliero!
Ah di scoprire il vero
ogni mezzo si cerchi, io sento in petto
e di sposo e d'amico
il dover che mi parla:
disingannar la voglio, e/o vendicarla.[35]

35. How will I believe a knight capable of such dreadful crime? Ah, let us try and unveil the truth in any possible way; I feel the duty of a husband and of a friend both speaking in my heart. I want to undeceive and / or to avenge her.

Note that the last line has two 'authorized' readings in the sources, and that each one carries an entirely different meaning: the 1787 Prague libretto has 'e' (and), but Mozart corrects it to 'o' in the autograph score and the same reading is found in the Vienna 1788 libretto, as if Da Ponte had accepted the correction (whether as a narrative mistake or a misprint is impossible to say).

Why is this so important? Because it defines Don Ottavio's epistemic system (what the character knows and believes at this point). Donna Anna has just recognized the voice of Don Giovanni as that of her aggressor. In addition, she has renewed (after Act I, sc. 3) Ottavio's commitment to avenge her father. Ottavio hardly believes Don Giovanni capable of the crime and is divided between his obligations as a husband and as a friend. Therefore, if the reading is 'e', this means that Ottavio wants to pursue two contradictory actions at the same time: undeceive Anna (his duty as Giovanni's friend) and avenge her (his duty as Anna's husband-to-be): the result is a character in confusion, whose action is prevented by his own hesitations. However, if the reading is 'o', this points to a clear course of action: Ottavio will act in such a way as to *either* undeceive Anna *or* avenge her. That Mozart's correction reinforces the male attitude of Ottavio is quite interesting, especially bearing in mind the negative image of this character as fixed by the Romantic generation.

While the first example stresses the relevance of historical culture for a sound understanding of the references, this one concerning Ottavio indicates that the verbal structures are not simply to be understood as the raw material on which the composer builds his musical artefacts according to an expressive paradigm; they also define other structures of broader significance: in the present case, the epistemic system of Ottavio, a vital element of the plot. As musicologists, we are naturally prone to think about structures primarily in musical terms, and these are certainly of the utmost importance. And yet, they are not entirely 'autonomous' structures but rather establish a network of relations with any of the other structures within the work.

Before moving on to properly musical items, I should like to recall a passage from Carl Dahlhaus' *Drammaturgia dell'opera italiana* that summarizes the present methodological approach, and which we are now in a better position to fully appreciate:

> The thesis that locates into the music the fundamental and constituent element of the peculiar drama called opera – a thesis that goes well beyond the acknowledgment of the preponderance of music – entrusts to the dramaturgy of music the duty to define which relationships are established, case by case, between the music and the other partial factors converging in the composite artistic *opus*.
>
> To define these relationships means to determine a hierarchy with different degrees of prominence and subordination. One can in fact take for granted, even before detailed analysis, that the relationship (the proximity or distance) between music and *fabula* or plot, music and conceptual structure of the drama, music and the constellation of the characters, music and scenic action, music and active or expressive-contemplative discourse, music and 'inner action', music and staging, will be extremely different, when we examine both each individual case (an individual opera or type), and the global phenomenon (i.e. "opera theatre" as a whole or by genre).[36]

The task of the analyst, then, is to determine a hierarchy with different degrees of prominence and subordination (proximity or distance) between music and any of the other parameters (plot, conceptual structure, constellation of characters, scenic action, active or expressive-contemplative discourse, 'inner action', and staging).

In the lines of recitative quoted above, the function of music is subordinate to stage action as carried on by the verbal text or by the para-text. One should add that the effectiveness of the action is less dependent on the work of the composer (*i.e.*: on the musico-dramatic text of the simple recitatives) than on the quality of performance (delivery, body language, etc.).

36. C. Dahlhaus, *Drammaturgia dell'opera italiana in Storia dell'opera italiana,* L. Bianconi and G. Pestelli eds., vol. 6 Teorie e tecniche, immagini e fantasmi, Turin: EdT musica, 1988, p. 83. Also in English in the volume *Opera in theory and practice, image and myth*, Chicago: University of Chicago Press, 2003.

The case is different with set pieces, where the hierarchy of the signifying elements is less easily established and where one tends to emphasize the relevance of specifically musical elements (melodic structures, rhythm, texture, style, mode, key, tone colour, etc.). The task is relatively simple in the case of a solo piece, typically an aria, where the verbal images (rarely numerous) are either amplified by the 'music setting' or, rarely, contradicted and, more often, rendered more elusive by the music. One classic case in *Don Giovanni* is 'Batti batti bel Masetto', where the enticing melody and texture anticipate from the very beginning the final result of Zerlina's seduction rather than reflecting the literal meaning of the words (which solicit physical punishment appropriate to the primitive mind of the peasant-girl).[37] A different case is 'Fin ch'han dal vino' generally known as the 'champagne' aria. The nickname comes from the 19th Century German tradition, only loosely related to Da Ponte.[38] In the original, Don Giovanni is instructing Leporello on how to arrange the orgy he wants to enjoy until next morning; in the German tradition, Giovanni starts out with a eulogy on champagne, usually performed with a glass in his hand, a tradition renewed in Milos Forman's movie by Ruggero Raimondi. In any case, the words are only to be understood through the libretto because the tempo indication *presto* (more often performed *prestissimo*) prevents any understanding whatsoever in performance. It is true, however that the extreme characterization through the frenzied rhythm conveys a musical portrait of Don Giovanni which transcends the text and has rightly become his musical emblem.

The interpretation of solo pieces has presented more problems (or presumed problems) in those cases where the prominence of the purely musical element – such as, for instance, virtuosic figuration for vocal display – prevails over the expressive (*i.e.* rational) paradigm. Various rhetorical artifices have been employed to

---

37. Another case within Mozart corpus is 'S'altro che lagrime' (Tito, No. 21) on which see my essay *L'ultima aria di Mozart su testo di Metastasio*, in *Studi su Mozart e il Settecento / Studies on Mozart and the 18th Century*, Lucca, L.I.M., pp. 1-18.

38. Rochlitz has the incipit 'Offne die Keller! / Wein soll man geben' etc. I find the, 'Champagne' *verbatim* in the late edition by Wittman (see above, f. 27), p. 49: 'Treibt der Champagner / das Blut erst im Kreise'. The first record of the term is probably much earlier but I have not been able to trace it.

explain these apparent (or partial) incongruences, but it is wise to accept that in opera, as elsewhere in the theatre, the element of the spectacular *per se* is occasionally placed at the top of the semiotic hierarchy, while the rational element becomes, even if temporarily, subordinate.

Let us examine, finally, the case in which more of the constituent elements of the *opus* come together in an entangled mix: ensembles and, especially, complex ones, such as the famous Sextet 'Sola sola in buio loco' in Act II. Ensembles in general present a sectional character: each phase is distinguished from the previous one through different devices, stylistic, tonal, textural etc. At the same time, the piece maintains a general level of unity, if nothing else because it begins and ends in the same key. 'Sola sola' is staged in the darkness of the night (be it real or symbolically presented on stage) where the characters can barely see each other (more precisely, they pretend to see, or not to see, according to the expository needs). Leporello, disguised as Don Giovanni, is trying to escape Elvira unnoticed and leaves her alone on one side of the closed garden while groping his way out through one of the doors which are found along the wall. The section is entrusted to two separate quatrains (one for each character), tonally moving from the E flat to its dominant. The Elvira and Leporello sections are melodically and texturally distinct, as are the two characters, differently portrayed in their parallel human weaknesses (Elvira scared to be alone in the darkness, Leporello scared to be discovered). The next section, keeping the original tempo Andante, articulates a totally new ethos with the entrance of Don Ottavio and Donna Anna in mourning dress. Again, there are two quatrains and two characterizations, but this time they are connected by a pervasive accompaniment complex (based on vl I and II combined). Don Ottavio, the first to speak, is introduced by a short modulatory bridge to D major and his section is intended to portray a dignified, and yet intense, attempt to console Donna Anna's grief; the latter prevails when, at the end of Ottavio's paragraph, the musical phrase ends suddenly in D minor rather than the expected major (the following sixteen bars – developmental in character and harmonically unstable – lead to a conclusion also in the minor but now C minor (relative minor to E flat); it is here that Mozart places the second change of key signature (from the two sharps of D major to three flats) which will last until the end of the piece.

The end of the Ottavio and Anna section and the beginning of the next is marked motivically by a new chromatic descent on a sighing (or perhaps 'suspenseful') figuration which, after a triple repetition, leads to a three-bar phrase ending on the dominant of C minor. This passage (only nine bars long) returns the attention to Elvira and Leporello (in disguise) who are groping their way in different sections of the stage: they will meet at the same time as they bump into Masetto and Zerlina entering onstage: the mutual surprise, linked with the recognition of the supposed Don Giovanni is marked out by a deceptive resolution from the dominant of C minor to the tonic of C major, immediately followed by i-iv-i.

The next section encloses the recognition of Don Giovanni/Leporello while Elvira implores mercy for him ('È mio marito'). Though the section is mainly characterized by the new chordal element functional to the screams 'No, no no!' and 'Morrà' (He will die!), it is also connected to the previous one by the aforementioned chromatic descent (found both in the accompaniment of vl I and in Elvira's part). At the end of this section (reaching G minor at bar 98), Don Ottavio is ready to kill Don Giovanni/Leporello but is prevented from doing so because of the next revelation. We find here a sudden change of texture, dynamics and musical gestures: Leporello discloses his identity and begs for mercy: a degree of motivic continuity is defined here, too, in the insinuating chromatic line of Leporello (G-A flat-G-F sharp-G: 'Perdon perdono, signori miei') as well as in the chromatic descending line, now entrusted to the winds and rhythmically modified so as to steer the expression from suspense to acceleration towards an inevitable ending.

At bar 113, after the sixteen bars of 'revelation', a new paragraph begins, introduced again by a harmonic surprise: the diminished 7th chord on VI (E flat/G/B flat/D flat) – This short section portrays the surprise of the five characters who sing homo-rhythmically to a new texture; however, the accompaniment includes, as a sort of motivic coda, the descending chromaticism in its original form. This final section of the Andante ends on the dominant of the local tonic C minor, with a pedal-point which precedes a sudden return to the tonic, E flat major.

We are at bar 130 of the Andante and at the beginning of the 147 bars of the Molto Allegro, a section which remains close throughout to the tonic/dominant regions, employs full instrumentation, with *clarini* and timpani, and is expanded through a combination of motivic variation, rhythmic invention, textural juxtapositions and a pre-final contrapuntal section *a voci sole*.

This passage has been the subject of a controversy, which is important not so much in itself but for its methodological implications. The object of discussion is the identification of the respective hierarchical positions of the different media and their functional relationship. In other words, is the musical element justified in relation to the verbal text and/or to the dramatic functions? Which considerations come first, those having a scenic relevance or those about the music *per se*?

For the sake of would-be objectivity, I will report the ideas of the rival parties as A and B.

According to critic A, the harmonic connection between the Andante and the Molto Allegro is rather unusual (A also finds that it is somewhat unsuccessful, in that it represents a sudden and inadequately prepared return to the tonic). Critic A substantiates his first remark on the basis of a thorough investigation of the Mozartean repertoire (and of relevant contemporary operas by other composers). Moreover, A has ascertained that similarly unusual harmonic passages may sometimes be found, albeit infrequently, in instrumental music by Mozart. From the dramatic point of view, on the other hand, A does not find any justification in the libretto for the 'sudden' harmonic passage.[39] This is because the dramatic 'surprise' (that might justify, or even require, a harmonic quirk of some sort) does not occur at bar 131, but earlier on, after Leporello's revelation (bar 113). The beginning of the Molto

39. This leads to the inference that Mozart borrowed his harmonic solution from the realm of instrumental music rather than relating it functionally to the stage situation.

allegro only presents the 'complementary' texts of Leporello, on the one hand, against all the rest, on the other:

> LEPORELLO:
> Mille torbidi pensieri
> mi si aggiran per la testa;
> se mi salvo in tal tempesta
> è un prodigio in verità!
>
> TUTTI GLI ALTRI:
> Mille torbidi pensieri
> mi si aggiran pel cervello,
> che disordine è mai quello,
> che impensata novità.[40]

These lines are not 'active' (*i.e.*: conveying action) but rather 'reflective'.[41] Therefore, claims critic A, no action is actually under way to justify the harmonic turn.

According to critic B, the harmonic passage might well be unusual but it is not is not especially 'sudden', especially if compared with previous harmonic shocks in the same piece. After all, although the tonal connection is relatively remote, the last chord of the Andante (G/B natural/D) has a harmonic link with E flat major in its mediant G. On the other hand, critic B locates the possible justification for this 'pace change' (defined not only by harmony but, even more conspicuously, by tempo, texture and rhythm) not so much at the level of stage action proper, but more with reference to the epistemic system, as defined above. Up to this point, the characters have acted 'as if' Leporello were Don Giovanni. Here, they enter into a new state of reality and, conversely, Leporello reverts to his true identity. It is true that the 'revelation' and the immediate reaction to it occur in the sixteen bars before, but equally true is that in opera (and spoken theatre as well) dramatic time does not aim at realism but is more often

40. LEPORELLO: Thousand dark thoughts turn around in my mind; if I save myself in this storm it is really a miracle. ALL OTHERS: Thousand dark thoughts turn around in my brain; what a disorder, what unforeseeable event.

41. On these terms and their theoretical implications see J. Platoff, *Musical and Dramatic Structure in the Opera Buffa Finale*, in *Journal of Musicology*, VII, 1989.

than not 'symbolic'. In other words, a certain symbolic amount of time is allowed between the revelation and its consequences. According to critic B, then, there is enough justification within the dramatic exposition for the unusual (but not necessarily shocking) return to the tonic.

It would be futile to establish who is right and who wrong.[42] The matter possibly boils down to different harmonic perception, taste and sensibility. But I would like to move on from here and consider whether the controversy touches upon a fundamental point or, rather, risks losing sight of more intriguing aspects of this famous piece. The Molto Allegro (lasting in most performances a little more than two minutes) has the character of a final climax owing to its scoring, acceleration with respect to the previous movement, rhythmic figuration, contrapuntal disposition and colour. By considering it 'reflective' (in the sense that no 'action' properly takes place but only 'reflection' on previous action), we overlook the fact that the verbal element might well represent the initial impetus but soon loses its importance with respect to the architectural development of the piece (not least, because the repetition time-and-again of the same words implies an exhaustion of their communicative function).

The piece, despite its tonal stability (which might be judged uninteresting compared to the previous sections), represents a compositional *tour de force* exactly because Mozart limits himself to restricted harmonic resources, while focussing on different ones. I surmise that the hierarchy of the Andante section, based on the pre-eminence of the verbal text and on the exposition of relevant dramatic elements, is here reversed: text and drama become a subsidiary, or even a decorative, function of compositional display, a 'spectacularization' of Mozart's skill. If the section is indeed of some consequence from the standpoint of

42. Critic A is J. Platoff and for his arguments see *Operatic Ensemles and the problem of the* Don Giovanni *sextet*, in *Opera Buffa in Mozart's Vienna*, M. Hunter and J. Webster eds., Cambridge: Cambridge University Press, 1997, pp. 378-405; critic B is this writer and my arguments and methodological approach are synthesized in the same volume within the essay *Analysis and Dramaturgy: Reflections towards a Theory of Opera*, pp. 311-339: 336 and f. 47.

dramatic exposition, this is due more to its 'aural' build-up than to the expression of the words' meaning. In any case, the 'affekt' here is 'confusion' more than anything else, symbolically represented through an artful musical game.

Let us consider briefly the consequences of this interpretation from the point of view of musical form *per se*. James Webster has shown convincingly that verbal structures are by themselves a nesting system of expectations with which the composer might or might not choose to comply: sometimes he does, sometimes he does not.[43] In the present case, we can read a degree of observance of the verbal implications, but also a degree of deviation on account of musical considerations.

Let us reconsider the piece in terms of its imprints of characterization: in the very beginning the piece is clearly sectional, albeit in different degrees: Elvira and Leporello definitely mirror this, as do Anna and Ottavio, but less than the former couple; we notice, in fact, that their two sections are unified by the accompaniment figures of vl I and II combined, which run through the two sections despite (or perhaps in compensation for) the tonal movement away from D major (Ottavio) through the sudden modal shift at the beginning of Anna's paragraph (D minor) towards the final goal of C minor. At this point, after the expository speeches of the four characters, a complication corresponding to a dialogic phase begins. This is characterized by a high number of 'surprises' (both visual/narrative and harmonic). The potential risk of formal dispersion is counterbalanced by Mozart through the motif first heard after the end of Anna's speech: the chromatic descent that we named 'sighing-' or 'suspense-' figuration (we find it at bars 61, 76, 90, 121 and also, in varied form, at bars 99 ff. in the woodwinds). The whole dialogic section of the Sextet is unified by this motif. Note that it is associated with Elvira at its first presentation ('È mio marito', and especially 'pietà pietà pietà' which doubles the violins: bars 78-79 and again 94). Note also, however, that although the figuration carries at first an expressive function, it loses it

43. See in particular J. Webster, *The Analysis of Mozart's Arias*, in *Mozart Studies*, C. Eisen ed., Oxford: Clarendon Press, 1991.

progressively along the way and assumes a different one which is primarily, I think, of formal significance. In theoretical terms, this means that, even within one and the same piece, the hierarchical relations change according to need: expression is a concern, but formal cohesion also engages the attention of the composer.

Finally, on the largest scale, the only unifying element of the Sextet is tonality. This is, on the one hand, a very precise element (in tonal terms) and, on the other, a rather unbalanced one, at least from a merely formal point of view. It is unbalanced in favour of the Molto allegro (a *stretta*), which is not only much longer than the home-key definition area (147 vs. 13 bars) but compositionally and aurally more committed and articulated. Of course, this observation only assumes the status of aesthetic criticism if we take it for granted that formal 'balance' is a value in itself. If, instead, the primary goal is the creation of a climax, the lack of balance becomes a functional resource. The sextet is such an imposing piece that Edward G. Dent thought that it might have been conceived as a finale within a four-act structure.[44] He was wrong about the four acts but the piece certainly marks the end of the 'peripeteia', after which the 'catastrophe' begins. In this sense its articulatory function is justified not so much by the structure of the sextet, but by the larger narrative functions of the opera as a whole.

* * *

What have been exposed are different ways to approach this opera, using types of discourse characteristic of different historical periods. After the two original *Don Giovanni* productions under Mozart's control, the most immediate interpretation of the opera should be recognized in the shameless theatrical adaptation, the *frei Bearbeitung* by Rochlitz. Then came the literary transfiguration by Hoffmann, a step in many ways original and polemical towards its immediate past, but also prepared for by the new theatrical taste of the 19th Century German bourgeoisie. After this, a curious mixture of respect for the original text and desire to 'upgrade' it to the

44. Dent E.J., *Mozart's operas: a critical study,* Oxford: Clarendon Press, 1947, p. 168.

level of Mozart's music came together in the ephemeral if ambitious initiative towards a 'definitive' *Don Juan* text.

One might easily ironize today on the apparent naiveté of the quest for a universal German standard text; in reality, that micro-history bears witness to the central function of Mozart's music within a process of cultural identification – paradoxically in a time of flourishing philology in other quarters of German culture. Of course, *Don Giovanni* is not *Don Juan*, but no other cultural tradition was as influential in shaping the critical image of the opera as the German one.

The characteristic element of today's Western culture is probably its lack of any focal point, and this makes virtually any *Don Giovanni* possible, provided that it offers at least a trace of 'newness'. It is a fluid situation, but no doubt *Don Giovanni* will survive it brilliantly.

THE ACT IV FINALE OF *LE NOZZE DI FIGARO*: DRAMATIC AND MUSICAL CONSTRUCTION[1]

James Webster

The entire institution of musical analysis is oriented conceptually towards instrumental music. (Recent studies of popular music may perhaps be an exception.) Moreover, the vast majority of analyses of instrumental music have been devoted to individual movements (or much shorter passages), and have tended to ignore both the large-scale coherence of multi-movement works, and questions of interpretation or meaning. As regards vocal music: even with respect to the privileged repertory of Mozart's operas, most recent analytical studies have been devoted to individual numbers or sections (and to the now contested topic of 'tonal planning'), and the majority are more nearly formal than contextual.[2] To be sure, formal analysis can discover many relations 'in' the notes, and these may be suggestive for interpretation, for example in Carl Schachter's analysis of Donna Anna's accompanied recitative and aria in Act I of *Don Giovanni*, or mine of the Countess's 'Porgi amor' in *Le nozze di Figaro*.[3] The latter was intended as a demonstration of the analytical method of *multivalence*: the thesis that in opera the relations among the fundamental domains of music, text, and action are flexible, the temporal patterns among them being sometimes temporally congruent,

---

1. In addition to the International Orpheus Academy in March 2008, versions of this study were presented at Harvard University in 2005, the annual meeting of the Society for Music Theory in 2006, and the Faculty of Music, Cambridge, in 2008.
2. On Mozart opera analysis see James Webster, 'Mozart's Operas and the Myth of Musical Unity', in: *Cambridge Opera Journal* 2 (1990) 2, pp. 197–218; Webster, 'The Analysis of Mozart's Arias', in: Cliff Eisen (ed.), *Mozart Studies*, London 1991, pp. 101–99.
3. Schachter, 'The Adventures of an F#: Tonal Narration and Exhortation in Donna Anna's First Act Recitative and Aria', in: *Theory and Practice* 16 (1991), pp. 5–20; Webster, 'Mozart's Arias', pp. 151–69.

contributing to the advancement of the plot in concert, at other times independent or even incompatible.[4]

In fact, however, no operatic number can be adequately understood unless the context is taken into account.[5] The latter includes (but is not limited to) the social and cultural milieu in which the work was created and produced; the libretto and ideational content; conventions of genre and plot, and of 'types' of character, aria, and ensemble; which characters sing and with what motivation; the dramatic context; performative aspects (including not only what singers do, but the vicissitudes of different versions and stagings) — and beyond, to the role the number plays in our view of the work as a whole.[6] Many of these aspects cannot be analyzed at all, in any ordinary sense.[7] Hence, although any operatic number can be analyzed, its form — that is, the resolution of one's analytical results into a coherent image that can be described in prose or represented in a diagram — remains fluid and contingent.

In short, operas are fundamentally different from works of absolute music, a category dependent on the concepts of the perfect, timeless artwork and the single, visionary author of genius.[8] Not only the methods associated with the analysis of abso-

4. The concept and method were developed by Harold S. Powers, in an unpublished study of Verdi's *Otello* presented at a Verdi-Wagner conference at Cornell University in 1984 (for the published papers see Carolyn Abbate and Roger Parker (eds.), *Analyzing Opera: Verdi and Wagner*, Berkeley 1989). For detailed expositions see Webster, 'Mozart's Arias'; Webster, 'The Form of the Finale of Beethoven's Ninth Symphony', in: *Beethoven Forum* 1 (1992), pp. 25–62.

5. Webster, 'Understanding Opera Buffa: Analysis = Interpretation', in: Mary Hunter and James Webster (eds.), *Opera Buffa in Mozart's Vienna*, Cambridge 1997, pp. 340–77.

6. This is not to endorse the older view that an 18th-century number-opera can be profitably *analyzed* as a whole, as in Siegmund Levarie's notorious representation of *Figaro* in its entirety as a single four-chord progression; see his *Mozart's 'Le nozze di Figaro': A Critical Analysis*, Chicago 1952, pp. 233–45.

7. Admittedly, the import of 'ordinary' can be contested; for an expansive view of operatic analysis, notably as regards dramaturgical aspects, see Sergio Durante, 'Analysis and Dramaturgy: Reflections towards a Theory of Opera', in: *Opera Buffa in Mozart's Vienna*, pp. 311–39.

8. Carl Dahlhaus, *The Idea of Absolute Music*, transl. Roger Lustig, Chicago 1989. Today, the proportion even of 18th- and 19th-century instrumental works that are accepted as 'absolute music' is increasingly small; some critics query whether there is any such category.

lute music, but the very traditions and ideologies that animate and sustain such analysis — notably their grounding in 'architectonic' formal types, the concept of 'tonal planning', and the search for unity — are suspect in the multifarious and contingent world of opera. Difficult as it may seem, analysts should therefore attempt to develop 'idiomatic' methods for opera, and should avoid the uncritical use of terms and concepts drawn from traditional instrumental analysis.

In this study I shall present some aspects of an analysis (in other respects still in progress) of the finale of Act IV of *Le nozze di Figaro*. However, as just noted, any such analysis must account as well for the context: at a minimum, the dramatic (and to some extent generic) significance of the action, in terms of the opera as a whole. I therefore begin with a brief summary of the plot and its significance.[9]

* * *

In *Figaro*, to modify slightly Wye Jamison Allanbrook's reading, the dramatic theme is the realization of human affection in society.[10] The action takes place within a social context (18th-century feudalism) that is dominated by conflicts of class and sex.[11] Notwithstanding Da Ponte's and Mozart's de-emphasizing of the overtly political aspects of Beaumarchais's play, class distinctions — Figaro and Susanna are comic servants; the Count and Countess, upper-class and at least potentially *seria*; Bartolo and Marcellina, *mezzo carattere* — remain at the heart of the action. For example, the Count exploits his rank to foster his attempted seduction of Susanna and to manipulate the outcome of Marcellina's suit against Figaro, and in Acts III–IV

9. This following section of this essay is condensed from Jessica Waldoff and James Webster, 'Operatic Plotting in *Le nozze di Figaro*', in: Stanley Sadie (ed.), *Wolfgang Amadè Mozart: Essays on his Life and his Music*, Oxford 1996, pp. 250–95 (here, pp. 255–64; Example 1 (below) is reproduced from pp. [260–61]).

10. *Rhythmic Gesture in Mozart: 'Le nozze di Figaro' and 'Don Giovanni'*, Chicago, 1983) pp. 73–75, 103–16, 127–31, 145–48, 170–85, 193–94.

11. Günter Reiss, 'Die Thematik der Komödie in "Le nozze di Figaro"', in: *Mozart-Jahrbuch* 1965–66, pp. 164–78; Frits Noske, *The Signifier and the Signified: Studies in the Operas of Mozart and Verdi*, The Hague 1977, ch. 2.

Example 1. Le nozze di Figaro: Development of the principal plots. from Jessica Waldoff and James Webster, 'Operatic Plotting in Le nozze di Figaro, in Stanley Sadie (ed.), Wolfgang Amadè Mozart: Essays on his Life and his Music, Oxford 1996, pp. [260–61], by permission of Oxford University Press

	Figaro and Susanna			Count and Countess			Marcellina and Bartolo	Cherubino
	Susanna *v.* Count	Figaro *v.* Count	Susanna *v.* Figaro	Count *v.* Susanna	Count *v.* Countess	Countess *v.* Count		
ACT 1								
Nos. 1-3 Figaro, Susanna	X	X	*X*	(X)				
Nos. 4-5 Marcellina							X	
Nos. 6-7 Cherubino, Count	X			X	X			X
Nos. 8-9 Figaro		X		(X)				*X*
ACT 2								
No. 10 Countess						X		
Nos. 11-12 Cherubino	(X)	X		(X)		(X)		X
Nos. 13-14 + Finale §1 Count, Countess	(X)	(X)			X	X		X
Finale §§2-3 + Susanna	X	(X)			↘ *X* ↙ (joining Count v. Countess and Countess v. Count)		(X)	
Finale §§4-5 + Figaro		X		X			(X)	(X)
Finale §§6-7 + Antonio		X		X				*(X)*
Finale §8 + Marcellina etc.				X			X	
ACT 3								
Nos. 16-17 Susanna, Count	X	(X)		X	(X)	(X)		
No. 18 Sextet	X	X	*X*	(X)			*X* (circled)	
Nos. 19-21 Countess, Susanna	(X)				(X)	X		
Finale	(X)	(X)		X		(X)		(X)
ACT 4								
Nos. 23-7 Figaro, Susanna		(X)	X					
Finale §§1-2 Cherubino, Count		(X)	(X)	X		(X)		X
Finale §§3-5 Figaro, Susanna		X	*X* (circled)	X	(X)	(X)		
Finale §§6-7 Count, Countess					↘ *X* (circled) ↙ (joining Count v. Countess and Countess v. Count)			
Finale §8 *lieto fine*								

The horizontal rows correspond to the 'segments' of the action (see p. 256); they are identified in terms of the familiar concerted muscial numbers for convenience only (the recitatives are often of equal or greater importance).

Actions expressing the overall theme of reconciliation are indicated in *italic boldface*; those that conclude an entire line of action are encircled.

Parentheses indicate either that the subplot is secondary, or that, although it is primary, its agent is not present (e.g. , §§2-3 and 6-7 of the Act 2 finale revolve around Cherubino, but he has long since escaped).

When the same characters are shown as belonging to more than one subplot , the distinction concerns the identity of the active agent (e.g., in the 'Figaro and Susanna' plot, the first column, 'Susanna *v.* Count', relates to her initiatives to frustrate him, in the 'Count and Countess' plot, the column 'Count v. Susanna' refers to his attempted seduction of her.

the Countess is profoundly ambivalent at having to enlist her maidservant's aid in scheming to regain her husband's affection. Mozart inscribes such distinctions into the music; for example, in 'Se vuol ballare', Figaro's vow to foil the Count is dramatized by his juxtaposition of a relatively crude minuet (normally an upper-class dance) and a middle-class contredanse.[12] Sexual conflict is equally important, in various guises: power (the Count's desire for Susanna, and her vulnerability), jealousy (the Count vs. the Countess and, in Act IV, Figaro vs. Susanna), female solidarity (the Countess and Susanna vs. the Count; also, in Act IV, Marcellina and Susanna vs. Figaro), legal and financial obligations vs. affection (Marcellina vs. Figaro), and so forth.

The action of *Figaro* comprises four distinct plots: three involving couples — Figaro and Susanna, the Count and Countess, Marcellina and Bartolo — and one centering around Cherubino and his desire.[13] Each of the three plots involving a couple culminates in a prominent scene of reconciliation (see Example 1).

12. Allanbrook, pp. 79–82, 123–24; Stefan Kunze, *Mozarts Opern*, Stuttgart 1984, pp. 240–45.

13. Of course, other analyses of the action are possible: for example, according to 'opposed' sets of characters, as in Hans Ludwig Scheel, '"Le Mariage de Figaro" von Beaumarchais und das Libretto der "Nozze di Figaro" von Lorenzo Da Ponte', in: *Die Musikforschung* 28 (1975) 2, pp. 159–60, and in John D. Drummond, *Opera in Perspective*, Minneapolis 1985, pp. 195–201; or the devices of comedy and stagecraft.

The mainspring of the action is Figaro's and Susanna's wish to be married, which, 'by definition', encounters obstacles. (Otherwise there would be no drama.) The Count, hoping to seduce Susanna, seeks to delay the wedding; hence she and Figaro must oppose him, by various stratagems. Meanwhile, a second aspect of the Figaro/Susanna plot comes to the fore in Act IV: his jealousy and lack of trust, and her 'teaching him a lesson'. This is no gratuitous comic enrichment; on the contrary, because it necessitates their making-up in the finale, it is crucial to the opera's dramatization of its theme.

Da Ponte's and Mozart's sympathetic portrayal of the Countess elevates the conjugal relationship between her and the Count into a second main plot, comparable in importance to the one involving Figaro and Susanna. As is common with such paired plots, the two are at once analogous and contrasted. Among the similarities are that both Figaro and the Countess conspire against the Count by means of assignation-letters and disguise, and that both women excite greater sympathy than their men, and each teaches her man a lesson about trust. On the other hand, not only are the two couples of different classes, their relationships are fundamentally different: Figaro's and Susanna's motives primarily coincide, and he ultimately proves worthy of her, whereas the Count's philandering and unmotivated jealousy are strongly contrasted to the Countess's long-suffering nobility.

The complexity of this action is crucial to the opera's dramatization of its overall theme. To be sure, from Aristotle's time until well into the 20th century, critics and operatic 'reformers' alike have tended to associate multiple plots with what has been viewed as objectionable, even defective, in all drama, and especially in comedy. Nevertheless, just as multiple-plot staged dramas had flourished since the Italian Renaissance and the Elizabethan period,[14] multiple-plot operas became common in

14. Louise George Clubb, 'Italian Renaissance Comedy', in: *Genre* 9 (1976–77) 4, pp. 469–88; Richard Levin, *The Multiple Plot in English Renaissance Drama*, Chicago 1971. On dramatic plotting in general, with more attention to Continental practice than is found in other surveys in English, see Manfred Pfister, *The Theory and Analysis of Drama*, 2nd ed., transl. John Halliday, Cambridge 1988, ch. 6.

the mid-seventeenth century, and remained so in late 18th-century *opera buffa*. Da Ponte was well aware of this aspect of *Figaro*, as is evident from his preface to the printed libretto —

> In spite of all the study, diligence, and care taken by the composer and by me to be brief, the opera will still not be the shortest one ever put on in our theatre, for which we hope that excuse enough will be found in the variety of threads with which the action of this drama is woven, the vastness and grandeur of the same, and the multiplicity of musical numbers which had to be made ... to express step by step with diverse colors the diverse passions that rival each other.[15]

— with its delicious litotes, 'not the shortest [opera]'; *Figaro* was the longest and most complex work mounted in Vienna since Joseph II's founding of the German National Theatre there in 1778.

Owing to both its deep-seated conflicts of class and sex and the complexity of its action, the moments of reconciliation in *Figaro* are profoundly satisfying as dramatic resolutions. Indeed the opera includes more reconciliation scenes than have been recognized in any single reading. The three primary, large-scale ones — between Figaro and Marcellina (Act III sextet), Figaro and Susanna, and the Count and Countess (the latter two in the Act IV finale) — are prepared by numerous earlier events. For example, the much-discussed opening duettino between Figaro and Susanna moves from disagreement to harmony, on 'her' terms.[16] (They must 'make up' in the Act III sextet as well.) Similarly, the Countess's pardon of the Count at the end is prefigured in the third section of the Act II finale (B-flat, Allegro). Each of these moments of reconciliation is marked, as the culmination of a series of events that has been dynamically directed towards it. Not surprisingly, the primary moments of reconcili-

15. *Le nozze di Figaro ... da rappresentarsi nel teatro di corte l'anno 1786*, Vienna, 1786; transl. Daniel Heartz, *Mozart's Operas*, Berkeley 1990, p. 121 (quoted here with minor changes).

16. Levarie, *Figaro*, pp. 17–19; Noske, 'Verbal to Musical Drama: Adaptation or Creation?', in: James Redmond (ed.), *Drama, Dance, and Music*, Cambridge 1981, pp. 143–52; Webster, 'To Understand Verdi and Wagner We Must Understand Mozart', in: *19th-Century Music* 11 (1987–88) 2, pp. 183–84.

ation are concentrated towards the end of the respective plot-strands. Moreover, the differences of class, sex, and characterization among the three couples enable their actions collectively to represent an entire society, circumscribed within the little world of Almaviva's castle. As a result, the successive reconciliations of the two main couples at the end create an overwhelming climax. For all these reasons of plotting — and not owing to Mozart's music alone — the achievement of human affection is thus the fulfillment of what the reconciliations have implied: reconciliation becomes universal.

* * *

The Act IV finale of *Figaro* interests me in part precisely because it is *not* the famous finale of Act II, which has attracted the lion's share of analytical and critical attention, owing to its compelling, ostensibly sonata-form-like tonal structure, as well as to its coordination of tonal and dramatic events. In fact, however, its degree of congruence between action and music is weaker than has generally been supposed; in particular, the primary dramatic resolutions do not coincide with musical closure on the largest scale.[17] Both the temporary reconciliation between Countess and Count, and the denouement of the Cherubino subplot (when Figaro outwits the Count regarding his possession of the page's commission), arrive *not* at the end of the finale, *not* in the tonic, but well before the end, and in the dominant. By contrast, the final sections in E-flat are highly unsettled: two opposed groups of characters are embroiled in an overt conflict whose outcome is by no means clear, and the key of E-flat itself is projected in an unstable manner. Both aspects — resolution in the middle but outside the tonic; instability at the end — reflect dramatic (or dramatic-musical) requirements as much or more than purely musical ones. The Act IV finale, by contrast, has received relatively little attention, although it is fully the equal of its more highly regarded counterpart. However, as implied by operatic

17. Abbate and Parker, 'Dismembering Mozart', in: *Cambridge Opera Journal* 2 (1990) 2, 194–95; Webster, 'Myth of Unity', pp. 207–08.

theory, it can be adequately understood only by considering its dramatic and musical construction and meaning together.

In opera (to repeat) the fundamental domains of music, text, and action are multivalent. As has been known since the early 20th century, in *Figaro* there tends to be a correlation between the 'segments' of the action (the comings and goings of the characters and changes of scene)[18] and the keys of the various set-pieces: within a given segment, the set-pieces tend to be in closely-related keys, whereas the relation between the last number in a given segment and the first number in the following one tends to be remote.[19] (See Example 2, where the brackets above the staff denote the dramatic segments in this sense, those below the staff the successions of closely-related keys.)

18. On 'segments' see Jacques Scherer, *La dramaturgie classique en France*, 2nd ed., Paris, 1959), pp. 214–24; Pfister, ch. 6.

19. Hermann Abert, preface to the Eulenburg miniature-score edition (ed. Rudolf Gerber), Vienna 1926; widely discussed in the more recent literature.

Example 2. Le nozze di Figaro: Dramatic and tonal segmentation

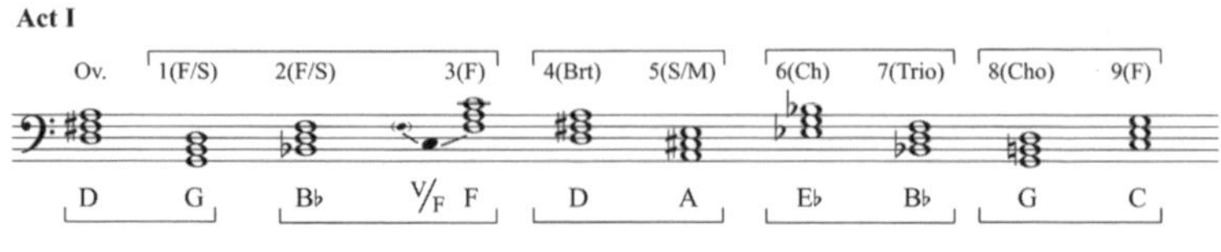

Act II
Finale
Ct, Cts +S
+F
+Ant −Ant
+M,B,B
10(Cts) 11(Ch) 12(S) 13(Trio) 14(S/Ch) 1 2/3 4 5 6 7 8ff.
E♭ B♭ G C G E♭ B♭ G C F B♭ E♭

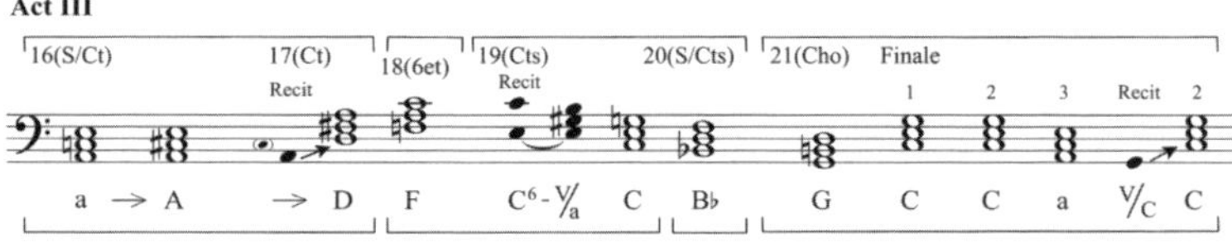

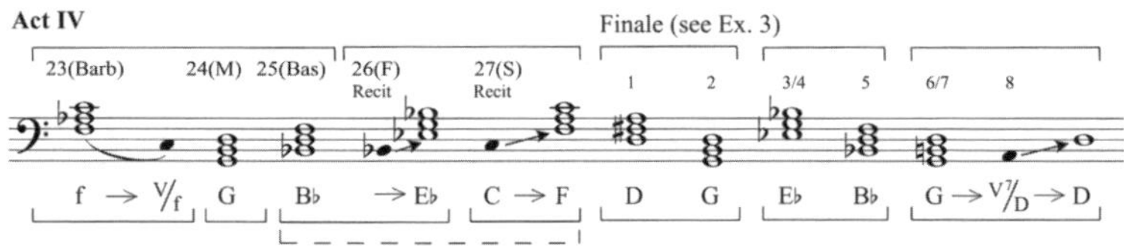

For example, in Act I the Bartolo-Marcellina subplot (nos. 4–5) stands in D and A, Cherubino's aria and the ensuing trio (nos. 6–7) in E-flat and B-flat, the denouement in G and C. However, these correlations are far from perfect: the first number for Figaro and Susanna in Act I is in G (following on the overture, in D), whereas the remaining two are in B-flat and F; the affective and conspiratorial action at the beginning of Act II (Countess, Susanna, and Cherubino; nos. 10–12) begins in E-flat and B-flat, but ends in G; the latter key (plus C) is maintained during the tense imbroglio (trio and duet; nos. 13–14) involving Cherubino in the closet. Characterological and typological requirements are often more important than tonal relations. For example, in the first segment of Act II the Countess sings 'Porgi amor' in the 'noble' key of E-flat, and Cherubino 'Voi che sapete' in the closely related key of B-flat, but Susanna must sing in a 'simple' maidservant's key, in this case G.[20] On yet the other hand, regarding the first three numbers it might be argued that a meaningful dramatic distinction exists between no. 1, in G, in which the differences between Susanna and Figaro are subtle rather than obvious and they end in harmony; and nos. 2–3, in B-flat and F, which bring the decisive impetus for the drama: Susanna informs her betrothed of the Count's intentions, and he resolves to thwart his master. (This ever-widening circle of potential interpretations is typical of the complexities of dramatic music, even on this relatively straightforward level of basic construction.)

In an analogous manner, recent critics, led by John Platoff, have replaced the older, simplistic pure-musical analyses of Mozart's finales with more dramatically sensitive and generically informed ones.[21] On the other hand, arias and ensembles, even those with multipart structures, usually present a more or less clear formal type. Since Mozart's finales also begin and end in the same key, it is least theoretically possible that they too exhibit musical form in some meaningful sense, even though the key-structure in the majority of Mozart's finales is not 'dynamic' or 'goal-oriented' as it is in *Figaro*, Act II. (Its 'strength' has always been attributed in large part, first, to the tonic–dominant polarity between E-flat and B-flat in its first three sections; and, second, to the systematic progression of keys by downward fifth from the sudden, remote G major at Figaro's entrance, back to E-flat at the entrance of Marcellina and her co-conspirators.) Nobody would deny the force of this progression, although the consensus today rejects any implication of a putative 'sonata form': Figaro's remote key does not initiate a 'development section', nor Marcellina's tonic

20. On these correlations between character-type and aria-key, see Webster, 'Mozart's Arias', pp. 107–14, 181–82.

21. Platoff, 'Musical and Dramatic Structure in the Opera Buffa Finale', in: *Journal of Musicology* 7 (1989) 2, pp. 191–230 (with references to earlier writings).

a 'recapitulation'![22] In any case, only one other mature Mozart finale places the penultimate section in the dominant key, namely *Così fan tutte*, Act II. Instead, we most often find the apparently non-teleological subdominant (*Figaro*, Act IV; *Don Giovanni*, Acts I and II; *Die Zauberflöte*, Act I), once the relative minor (*Die Zauberflöte*, Act II), and only once a remote key, the flat submediant (*Così*, Act I).

Now if, in a finale, the only sections in the tonic are the first and last, it scarcely matters what particular keys appear in between; in terms of tonality the only available formal type will be some kind of 'arch'. With respect to end-finales, this obviously works with respect to the final *stretta*, in which the concluding stable tonic correlates with dramatic closure (the plot winds up in concord, the characters in happy homophony). It may suit the middle section(s) as well, in which the dramatic high-points of conflict and complexity correlate with notionally unstable non-tonic keys, often remote ones. However, the action at the beginning of a finale is usually conflict-ridden and unstable; to this extent it does not correlate with the putative 'stability' of an opening tonic section (paradigmatic are *Figaro*, Acts II and IV; and *Don Giovanni*, Act I). A complex relation is often present at the denouement in an end-finale as well: although it may be locally stable and entail tonal resolution within the section in which it occurs, it is never in the tonic (that is reserved for the concluding *lieto fine*), and hence bears no one-to-one correlation with any putative 'tonal form'. (As we shall see, this relationship obtains in the celebrated forgiveness scene between Count and Countess in *Figaro*.)

For the sake of additional context, let us briefly examine the construction of the Act I finale of *Don Giovanni*, which begins and ends in C major. To be sure, the music moves by fifth at the beginning, but it does so in the *subdominant* direction: to F major and D minor (Giovanni's renewed attentions to Zerlina, Masetto's interruption, contredanse and minuet heard from

22. Admittedly, certain authorities such as Charles Rosen still insist on the relevance of sonata form in contexts such as this; see *The Classical Style* ..., expanded ed., New York 1997, pp. xxi–xxvi.

indoors, entry of the maskers), through B-flat (their prayerful invocation), to E-flat, the point of furthest remove (at the change of scene, to the interior of Giovanni's town-house). There are no implications of sonata form or even 'key-area form'.[23] However, when the maskers arrive indoors for 'Libertà!', Mozart abruptly returns to the opening key of C, followed by the three simultaneous dances in G, the crisis (beginning in E-flat and leading to the dominant of D minor), Giovanni's accusation of Leporello and his pursuers' unmasking, in F, and the final *stretta* in C. Nor do music and drama correspond at the primary division points: the change of scene is merely the final step flatwards, while the ensuing return to C accompanies merely the entrance of the maskers. On another level, although the dominant G might seem a tonally orthodox continuation for the following section, the excruciating musical, social, and dramatic tension of the three dances, 'senza alcun' ordine' (as Giovanni had commanded in his aria), is anything but orthodox. To be sure, the key-successions, exhibit a clear double-arch progression, including aspects of symmetry and a repeated use of E-flat as the key of furthest remove: (1) C–F–d → Eb | C; (2) C–G–Eb → V/d–F–C. Nevertheless, dramatic association, instrumental usage, and other non-formal factors seem to be primary, just as they are in the choice of aria-keys: for 'Libertà', the march/majesty topic and the return of the trumpets and timpani dictate C major; the minuet is deployed symmetrically in the two closely-related keys a fifth on either side of it; the only prominent minor key is D, whose significance in this finale is more nearly associational than formal; and so forth. Nor can this be called 'rondo form', for which the requisite thematic returns (and many other factors) are lacking. Yet what alternative formal type is available?

* * *

23. Leonard G. Ratner's term 'key-area form' (adopted by Allanbrook) describes the general two-part harmonic plan underlying most 18th-century movements: I—V || x—I. Sonata form is (from this point of view) merely one subtype of key-area form; the latter concept is in fact often more useful in operatic analysis.

Let us now examine the Act IV finale of *Figaro* in detail (see the formal diagram in Example 3).

In fact, an A–B–A construction obtains on a number of levels:

	§§ 1–2	§§ 3–5	§§ 6–8
characters onstage[24]	many (focus: Ct/Cts)	few (focus: Sus/Fig)	many (focus: Ct/Cts)
'structure' of the action	confusion	focus	confusion → communal
musical meter	Duple	triple or compound	duple
tonality	Diatonic tonic (§ 1 only)	remote non-tonic (§§ 2–7)	diatonic tonic (§ 8 only)

However, one ought not generalize these observations into conclusions such as that the finale exhibits 'A–B–A *form*', or even that it is 'ternary'. In fact, non-congruencies exist even with respect to the parameters just mentioned. The parsings 'tonic—non-tonic—tonic' (musical sections 1, 2–7, 8) and 'diatonic—remote—diatonic' (sections 1–2, 3–5, 6–8) do not map directly onto each other. In this particular context, the diatonic aspect of G major seems more pertinent, because it corresponds more strongly with the distinctions among the foregrounded characters and the segmentation in the dramatic action. Put another way, sections 2 and 6–7 are at one and the same time 'foreign' and 'home': G is in this sense a transitional key, which leads from the tonic to remote areas, and then returns. (We will return to the functions of G below.)

The traditional marginalization of this finale entails the claim that it is more 'sectional', less dynamically through-composed,

24. Allanbrook (p. 173) and others interpret the differences in this category as establishing a distinction between 'public' and 'private' aspects of the action. This seems oversimplified; unlike for example at the end of Act III, there is no 'public' present, and in particular no chorus. Nevertheless, her discussion of sections 3–5 of this finale is the best in print (she devotes less attention to the remaining sections).

than the Act II finale.[25] (Perhaps this critique is related to the frequent criticism of Act IV in general, on the grounds that, except for the finale, it consists of arias only, with no ensembles.[26]) This claim is erroneous; the error is doubtless an uncritical corollary of critics' fixation on the supposedly sonata-form-like quality of the Act II finale. In fact, the majority of the sectional joins in Finale IV are run-on (signaled in Example 3 by arrows in the row 'Keys'), and the join between sections 6–7 is equally dynamic, because of the half-cadence on the dominant in the context of the minor mode. The first four sections are entirely continuous: nos. 1–2 are linked by a modulating transition from D to G (Example 4), nos. 2–3 by another modulating transition from G to E-flat via G minor (Example 5), and nos. 3–4 by an elided, run-on cadence at the end of Figaro's minuet (not shown). The only sections that end with a full stop on a prevailing tonic are the two primary sections for Figaro and Susanna (nos. 4 and 5; see Example 6); indeed, with the exception of the last measure of the opera, the only fermata on a concluding tonic comes at the end of section 4 in E-flat, when Susanna is still raving and only Figaro understands what is going on, i.e., at the point of maximum dissonance and complexity within their subplot.

More importantly, the implicitly symmetrical character of any 'ternary' reading is out of countenance with the dramatic drive towards reconciliation.[27] The Figaro/Susanna 'jealousy' subplot reaches back to the beginning of Act IV, the Count/Countess

[text continues on p. 115]

25. E.g., Allanbrook, p. 186: 'While the keys of the second-act finale shape a well-plotted key-area layout with a thrust to the dominant and point of furthest remove from the tonic, the keys of the fourth-act finale are [merely] grouped in pairs.... The center pair ... is not established by any motion of harmonic grammar'; Abbate & Parker, p. 195: 'The various subsections are so to speak merely *juxtaposed*, almost perfunctorily' (emphasis original).

26. E.g., Joseph Kerman, *Opera as Drama*, 2nd ed., Berkeley 1988, pp. 89, 101. For a corrective, see Allanbrook, pp. 157–77.

27. For an attractive reading of this finale in terms of its performative aspects, especially the 'play within a play' of the duping of the Count and its relation to the reconciliation between Susanna and Figaro (sections 2–5), see Alessandra Campana, 'The Performance of Opera Buffa: *Le nozze di Figaro* and the Act IV Finale', in: Stefano La Via and Roger Parker (eds.), *Pensieri per un Maestro: Studi in onore di Pierluigi Petrobelli*, Turin 2002, pp. 125–34 (although she says little about formal construction).

Example 3. Le nozze di Figaro, Act IV finale: Formal organization

Scene	[11]–12[1]		13	
Char's	Cts,Ch; Sus,Ct,Fig (exit Ch)		Fig	Sus,Fig
Plot-strands	Ch nuisance [end] … → →	Ct pursues Sus →		Sus teaches Fig a lesso (and he teaches her)
Action	Ch wants to kiss 'Sus' but kisses Ct instead; Ct intends to hit Ch but hits Fig. instead	'Sus' leads Ct on; Ct gives her a ring: 'Come with me'; Fig's anger; Ct/'Sus' exeunt	Fig's jealousy	Fig recognizes Sus; makes love to her as 'Cts' (she doesn't know he knows); h slap; his joy
Prosody	8; **-à**	7; **-or; -ar**	7; **-ò**	7; **-ò; -or**
Musical Section	**1** 1–50	**2** 51–108	**3**[3] 109–121	**4** 121–274
Tempo	Andante	Con un poco più di moto	Larghetto	Allegro molto
Meter	¢		3/4	
Keys	D →	G →	Eb →	
Tonic?	I	Other		
Relation?	Diatonic		Remote	
Formal type[4]	Sonata form	Sonata form (only brief TRS)[5]	[Minuet]	Exp + {TRSx2} (rondo aspects)
Closure	47, 50	100? 106?	121	272

1. Scene 11 continues from the preceding recitative; Scene 12 = the Count's entrance (m. 22).
2. The poetic discourse, the Count's hue and cry, and the musical changes imply that this scene begins at the beginning of the new musical section (so indicated, as 'Scena ultima', in NMA and other scores); the libretto, following dramaturgical convention, gives Scene 15 at the entry of the new characters, corresponding to m. 343.
3. The cadence of this section (downbeat of m. 121) is elided to the first bar of the following one. Allanbrook, *Rhythmic Gesture*, pp. 177 ff., argues that mm. 109–274

4	15[2]		
us,Fig; then Ct	Ct; tutti; (Cts)	Ct,Cts; tutti	Tutti
… → → [end] —— **R** … → →	Ct's jealousy & its undoing ——— **R**		
ig confesses he nows her; they rec- ncile; Ct seeks 'Sus'; ig and 'Cts' make ove; Ct's rage	Ct's hue & cry; all beg forgiveness, including 'Cts'; Ct refuses. —Cts enters; shock tutti	Ct begs forgiveness; Cts grants it; 'Ah tutti contenti'	<u>Lieto fine</u>
0; **-or**	8; **-er**; **-à**; **-ò**	6; **-ì**	8; **-ar**
 75–334	**6** 335–420	**7** 421–447	**8** 448–521
ndante	Allegro assai	Andante	Allegro assai
/8	¢		
b	G (–g –V/g 𝄐)	G →	V→D
			→I
	Diatonic		
xp ++ Dev+TRS}	Exp + TRS (recap → minor)	Double period: 10(4+6) + 11(4+7)	—V; —I 471; end
334		445	513 𝄐

constitute a single section, based on key, the minuet topic, and 'key-area form'; one could add to these criteria the maintenance of settenario and end-rhyme **-ò**.
4. The concept 'formal type' refers to the 'background' or 'generic' default form in terms of which the section may be understood; it must not be taken as an assertion that the section is 'in' the form in question. Cf. Webster, 'The Analysis of Mozart's Arias', pp. 114–22.
5. "TRS" = tonal return section; cf. ibid., pp. 118–19.

Example 4. Le nozze di Figaro, Act IV finale: mm. 44–54. Reproduced from Wolfgang Amadeus Mozart: Le nozze di Figaro (based on the Neue Mozart-Ausgabe), Bärenreiter 1976 (BA 4565a)

47
3̂
2̂
Sus.
tà! Ah ci ha fat - to un bel gua - da - gno col - la sua cu - rio - si -
La C.
tà! Ah ci ha fat - - - to un bel gua -
Il C.
tà! Ah ci ha fat - - to un bel gua -
Fig.
tà! Ah ci ho fat - to

48
1̂
(etc.)
Sus.
tà! Ah ci ha fat - to un bel gua - da - gno col - la sua cu - rio - si -
La C.
da - gno col - la sua cu - rio - - - si -
Il C.
da - gno col - la sua te - me - ri -
Fig.
un bel gua - da - gno col - la

49
Sus.
tà, col - la sua cu - rio - si - tà, col - la sua cu - rio - si - tà!
La C.
tà, col - la sua cu - rio - si - tà!
Il C.
tà, te - me - ri - tà, te - me - ri - tà!
(Si ritira.)
Fig.
mia cu - rio - si - tà, cu - rio - si - tà!)
I = V
51 Con un poco più di moto
Il Conte (alla CONTESSA)
Il C.
Par - ti - to è al - fin l'au -
G
53
Il C.
da - ce, ac - co - sta - ti ben

Example 5. Le nozze di Figaro, Act IV finale: mm. 95–114

La Contessa
(Entra a man destra.)
ii Conte
Fig.
La C.
Il C.
gen - te! È Fi - ga - ro: men vò! An - da - te an -
Il C.
(no 2)
(Si disperde pel bosco.)
da - te; io poi ver - rò.
I i E♭: V7
Scena XIII
FIGARO e SUSANNA.
Larghetto
Figaro
Fig.
Tut - to è tran - quil - lo e
I
Fig.
pla - ci - do; en - trò la bel - la

Example 6. Le nozze di Figaro, Act IV finale: mm. 260–84

I suddetti, poi IL CONTE.
Andante
Figaro (si mette in ginocchio.)
275
Fig.
Pa - ce pa - ce, mio dol - ce te - so - ro, io co -
f
p

278
Fig.
nob - bi la vo - ce che a - do - ro e che im - pres - sa o - gnor ser - bo nel

281
Susanna (ridendo e con sorpresa)
Sus.
La mia vo - ce?
Fig.
cor.
La vo - - ce che a -

plot all the way to the beginning of Act II, and even in its more recent guise (the Countess's decision to take over the conspiracy) to the middle of Act III. These strands of the action, and hence these dramatic resolutions, are thus independent of whatever form the finale might seem to have in its own right. On the contrary, as described, the overwhelming effect of the ending (taken in its entirety) is owing to the successive reconciliations of both primary couples — the rounding-off of both primary plot-strands. Indeed the first of these, when the Figaro/Susanna subplot reaches its definitive resolution, takes place not only in the putative 'middle' section but in a remote key; that is, in a harmonic situation that from a pure-musical view can only be construed as unstable. Again, as is to be expected in a multiple-plot drama, the two resolutions are at once similar and different. While the similarities are obvious, the differences are perhaps equally important: Susanna and Figaro are (effectively) alone, and nobody overhears them (this would appear, again, to be correlated with the remote B-flat, in its turn musically and dramatically linked to the 'Letter Duet' and both of their arias in Act IV).[28] By contrast, the Countess and Count play out their forgiveness in the presence of 'witnesses' — almost all the named characters of the opera — and in the diatonically related G major. These complementary differences enhance the overall effect: again, the entire little world of Almaviva's castle enters into a state of resolution.

In fact, the key of G major itself functions multivalently in this finale. The first tonal move is a fifth down, to the subdominant; there can be no question of a 'sonata' or 'key-area' form for the finale as a whole. Although in section 2 the excruciating imbroglio of section 1 is somewhat reduced, the characters are still in disguise and acting at cross-purposes, the Count is still pursuing 'Susanna', and the tempo speeds up, albeit with a reduction of the shortest notated values from demisemiquavers to semiquavers. That is, the notionally 'relaxed' subdominant here accompanies a sharper dramatic focus and a faster tempo. In the

28. Waldoff and Webster, pp. 264–74.

denouement this key functions even more multifariously: first, the very fast section 6 brings action and confusion (the Count's hue and cry, the remaining characters' emerging from the pavilions, the Countess's and Figaro's futile pleas for forgiveness, and the true Countess's very different plea, with its immediate transformation of the mood and the characters' understanding); secondly, the 'shock tutti'[29] in the parallel minor for all the men except Figaro, leading to a pause on the dominant; and finally a change of tempo to Andante and return to the major for the celebrated forgiveness scene (section 7). It is noteworthy that both sections are in the same key, despite the contrast in mood and tempo: since the resolution in section 7 is the direct outcome of the preceding imbroglio, Mozart presumably felt a need for tonal continuity even in an otherwise 'sectional' context where he would ordinarily have employed a tonal contrast. The choice of G as such was presumably based, again, not so much on 'musical form' as on appropriate tonal contrast, affect, and tessitura. (The only other closely-related major key is A, the dominant. However, this key could scarcely have followed directly from B-flat (whereas G/B-flat juxtapositions abound throughout the opera; cf. Example 2); the music as Mozart composed it might have been uncomfortably high for the Countess (Luisa Laschi), and perhaps altogether have strained excessively; and, as indicated above, the keys associated with the Count's and Countess's communal functioning are G (not A) and C.) Be all this as it may: as in section 2, and notwithstanding the epiphany of the reconciliation, the effect of the subdominant here is very different from the 'relaxation' that is ordinarily said to be its effect in an instrumental movement.[30]

[text continues on p. 121]

29. On the shock tutti, see Platoff, 'Opera Buffa Finale', pp. 219–22 (in this case, the maintenance of the fast tempo for the shock is unusual).

30. In recent decades this section has usually been taken as a hymn-like Adagio, in contrast to Mozart's marking 'Andante' (which in his time meant, literally, 'going'; neither fast nor slow). This inaccurate tempo both creates and reflects the modern understanding of the scene as the emotional climax of the opera, with profound and not always beneficial consequences for interpretation. See Richard Will, 'The Ambivalence of Mozart's Countess', in James P. Cassaro (ed.), *Music, Libraries and the Academy: Essays in Honor of Lenore Coral*, Middleton (Wis.) 2007, pp. 31–53.

Example 7. Le nozze di Figaro, Act IV finale: mm. 439–71

448
Allegro assai
Sus.
La C.
Que - sto gior - no di tor -
Barb.
Cher.
Marc.
Bas.
Il C.
Ant.
Fig.
Allegro assai
g
D: V7
452
men - ti, di ca - pric - ci, e di fol -
V
(i)

456
3̂
Sus.
La C.
li - a, in con - ten - ti e in al - le - gri - a so - lo a - mor può ter - mi -
Barb.
Cher.
Marc.
li - a, in con - ten - ti e in al - le - gri - a so - lo a - mor può ter - mi -
Bas.
li - a, in con - ten - ti e in al - le - gri - a so - lo a -
Il C.
li - a, in con - ten - ti e in al - le - gri - a so - lo a -
Ant.
Fig.
li - a, in con - ten - ti e in al - le - gri - a so - lo a -
p
sf
p
sf
V
I
460
3̂
2̂
Sus.
La C.
nar, so - lo a - mor può ter - mi -
Barb.
Cher.
Marc.
nar, so - lo a - mor può ter - mi -
Bas.
mor può ter - mi - nar, so - lo a - mor può ter - mi -
Il C.
mor può ter - mi - nar, so - lo a - mor può ter - mi -
Ant.
Fig.
mor può ter - mi - nar, so - lo a - mor può ter - mi -
f
sf
f
sf
I
V

464
Î
(etc.)
Sus.
La C.
nar. Spo - si, a - mi - ci, al bal - lo, al
Barb.
Cher.
Marc.
nar. Spo - si, a - mi - ci, al bal - lo, al
Bas.
nar. Spo - si, a - mi - ci, al bal - lo, al
Il C.
nar. Spo - si, a - mi - ci, al bal - lo, al
Ant.
Fig.
nar. Spo - si, a - mi - ci, al bal - lo, al
I
(etc.)
468
gio - co, al - le mi - ne da - te fo - co, da - te fo - co!
I
V

Then follows the concluding *stretta* (see Example 7). This section too has suffered from a kind of marginalization, as disappointingly short or conventional,[31] but it is in no respect disappointing and certainly not 'merely' conventional. (Not to mention that Mozart himself claimed that the shortest possible windup was the most effective one[32] — a principle, admittedly, that he did not always observe, for example in *Don Giovanni*, Act I, and *Così*, Act I; even in *Figaro*, Act II, the three concluding sections in E-flat together are long and highly repetitive, although the final Prestissimo alone certainly satisfies his dictum.) Most important from the present perspective, the concluding D major does not follow directly from the G major of section 7. The wonderful orchestral transition modulates to the dominant (the 'home' dominant, of course), and the *stretta* not only begins on this sonority, but also prolongs it at least through the end of the minor-mode shadow (m. 456), if not indeed all the way to the structural half-cadence in m. 471 (see again Example 7). The progression is thus not IV–I, as one often reads,[33] but IV–V–I, indeed IV–V^7–I: the pitch-class *g* is maintained unbroken through the orchestral transition, through to the downbeat of section 8. This is unusual — structural half-cadences of this kind are ordinarily pure triads — which is to say that the transition is 'through-composed', into the new beginning on V^7. The finale is thus more 'tightly' — more dramatically — organized towards

31. Abbate and Parker dismiss this section as 'a small coda, temporally insignificant'; Tim Carter, in *W. A. Mozart:* The Marriage of Figaro, Cambridge 1987, p. 121, calls it 'trite'. Allanbrook ('Mozart's Happy Endings: A New Look at the 'Convention' of the *lieto fine*', in: *Mozart-Jahrbuch* 1984–85, pp. 1–5) proleptically defended it against charges of this kind, but in terms of dramatic-musical convention, not of overall 'form'. On the necessity for 'communal' dramatic and musical closure at the end of an *opera buffa*, see Hunter, *The Culture of Opera Buffa in Mozart's Vienna*, Princeton 1999, pp. 225–26.

32. Letter to Leopold of 26 September 1781, *W. A. Mozart: Briefe und Aufzeichnungen*, vol. 3, Kassel 1963, p. 163; (translation mine): 'But then the major [mode] enters immediately *pianissimo* — which must go very fast — and the ending will make a lot of noise — and that is all that belongs at the end of an act — the more noise, the better — the shorter, the better — so that the audience doesn't get too cold to applaud.'

33. E.g., in Heartz, p. 150. (Allanbrook, p. 193, oddly calls this dominant 'artificial', presumably because it is not a key in its own right.)

the end than would be suggested by a mere recitation or diagram of the successive tonal centers.[34] This is a primary reason that the ending is so satisfying, 'despite' its brevity: the final tonic is grounded in the strongest possible manner, within the course of the *stretta* itself (unlike the dominant preparations for sections 2, 3, and 7, which precede and therefore lie outside these sections); the *lieto fine* (finally) calls forth an equally strong tonal resolution. (Perhaps its subliminal recalls of the overture, especially the rushing quaver motion that accompanies 'Corriam tutti', play a role as well.[35]) Although it is true that in all of Mozart's finales in which the penultimate section is not in the dominant (except *Così*, Act I), an organized transition leads from the penultimate section via the home dominant to the final section, the goal is usually a dominant triad with fermata, followed by the *stretta* beginning on the tonic, rather than the through-composed version found in *Figaro*.

* * *

I would now like to speculate briefly on the possibility of a Schenkerian analysis of this finale. I am of course aware that this may seem to go against the grain even of the relatively nuanced degree of revisionism I endorse regarding the bad old days of pure-musical opera analysis. In fact, however, for individual numbers (especially arias) the Schenkerian method is a powerful tool, especially when combined with a complementary focus on the 'high-note' construction of the vocal line.[36] And (to repeat) since the finale begins and ends in the same key, and since, as we have just seen, its final two sections are linked in a through-composed IV–V^7–I progression, the theoretical possibility of an underlying tonal voice-leading structure cannot be rejected out of hand.[37]

34. Webster, 'Myth of Unity', pp. 215–16.
35. Heartz, p. 150.
36. Webster, 'Aria Analysis', pp. 166–69.
37. For an analogous Schenkerian reading of a complex but mutually related series of numbers, see Schachter, '"E Pluribus Unum: Large-Scale Connections in the Opening Scenes of *Don Giovanni*', in Allen Cadwallader (ed.), *Essays from the Fourth International Schenker Symposium*, Hildesheim 2008, vol. 1, pp. 3–22.

Example 8. Le nozze di Figaro, Act IV finale: Schenkerian analysis

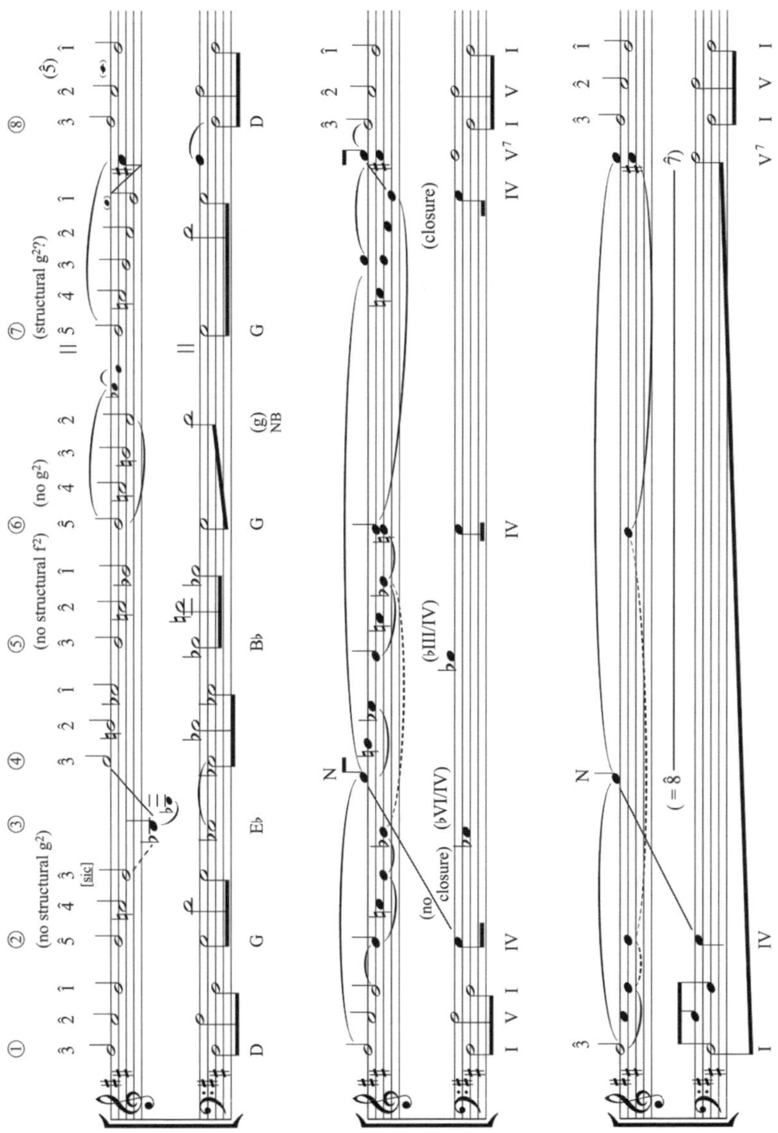

Example 8 presents a Schenkerian reading of the finale; the endings of the relevant sections and the ensuing transitions, which are relevant in this context, have been given in Examples 4–7. Example 4 shows the end of the initial section in D, which is unexpectedly in a full-dress sonata form ('unexpectedly', because of the dramatic confusion): second group beginning in m. 7, second half (beginning with the initial motive) in m. 22, recapitulation in m. 34, with reprise of mm. 10–11 in mm. 40–41. At the end, the high-note $f\#^2$ repeatedly descends by step to d^2. But the ending of section 2 is far less stable (see Example 5). Although it too is clearly based on sonata form as a type — second group beginning in m. 59, development in m. 80 — in distinction to section 1 it has no proper recapitulation. Instead, following the arrival on the home dominant in m. 97 and the cadence onto the tonic in m. 100, we have merely the 'out of countenance' byplay as Figaro intrudes on the couple, and 'Susanna's' hasty leave-taking. Moreover, there is no structural melodic descent: every time 'Susanna' cadences, she merely sings $\hat{3}$ in the melody; even the Count, whose last line does cadence on $\hat{1}$, cannot connect it to the preceding $\hat{3}$ by step. (My working hypothesis in such contexts is that the essential melodic motion must appear in the highest or leading vocal part(s); the bass register (except in an aria) and especially the orchestra do not 'count'.) This emphasis on $\hat{3}$ at the expense of $\hat{1}$ prevents meaningful closure. The dramatic pertinence of this instability is self-evident; in addition, that crucial $\hat{3}$ now instigates the modulation to the remote E-flat, by moving down to $\flat\hat{3}$ (G minor) and then to V^7–I in the new key. On a larger scale, the withheld closure in G powerfully motivates the full and unambiguous closure in the same key in the final reconciliation.

The long pair of sections in E-flat reaches harmonically and gesturally very strong closure (see Example 6). However, despite her repeated high-note g^2 (with its neighbor ab^2), seen three times in this brief excerpt alone, Susanna cannot cadence in this, her 'obligatory' register; the $\hat{2}$-$\hat{1}$ is always displaced an octave lower (this was so in earlier passages as well). Perhaps this correlates with the fact that she is still deluded, angry, not in control. Be this as it may, in the ensuing reconciliation section in B-flat (of which only the beginning is shown), by contrast, she repeatedly cadences strongly with $\hat{3}$-$\hat{2}$-$\hat{1}$ motion down from her high-note d^2. Although sections 4–6 begin with an exposition (section 4: mm. 121–39 + 140–75; section 5: mm. 275–97 + transition + 306–19; section 6: mm. 335–59 + 360–81 or –89), none executes a sonata-like form as a whole. Indeed, this formal type consistently recedes in importance during the course of the finale: no recapitulation in section 2, at most a key-area form in section 5, and at most an exposition in sections 4 and 6. The most complex formal type is associated with the greatest degree of dramatic complexity, while the drive towards resolution is associated with 'simpler' ones.

In the subsequent reconciliation between Count and Countess the harmonic and gestural closure is as strong as one could wish (Example 7), thus fulfilling the expectation created by its having been withheld in section 2. The only complication (if that is what it is) is that the structural melodic motion down from $d^2 = \hat{5}$ in m. 442–45 has no $c^2 = \hat{4}$ over the subdominant, this harmony instead supporting the final poignant rise to g^2. (d^2 is unambiguously established as the headnote in the Countess's first phrase, m. 425 [not shown], following on the Count's initial high-notes b–c^1.) In fact, however, weak articulations of $\hat{4}$ in a $\hat{5}$-line context are not uncommon. Or $\hat{4}$ may have occurred earlier, in the very clear $\hat{5}$-$\hat{4}$-$\hat{3}$-$\hat{2}$-$\hat{1}$ descents by the Countess in mm. 427–30 and the full ensemble in mm. 433–36, or at the V^7 in m. 438 (not shown); in the latter case, the background melody descends to $\hat{3}$ already in m. 439, which is picked up again in m. 434.

* * *

Now let us examine how and to what extent these sections, with their various high-notes and endings, fit together (see Example 8). The top system presents the apparent *Ursatz* for each section separately (the sections are identified by encircled Arabic numbers at the top). Section 1, as stated, has a clear *Ursatz* based on $\hat{3}$. Section 2, again as stated, has no convincing descent to the tonic; its structural motion instead comprises $\hat{5}$-$\hat{4}$-$\hat{3}$ in G, with the concluding *b* being transformed to *b*♭ and thus preparing the flat-side sections that follow. In the big duet section 4 in E-flat, I show a descending *Urlinie* from $\hat{3}$ (g^2), notwithstanding the registral difficulties alluded to above; as we shall see, this adjustment doesn't materially compromise any overall structure we may wish to discern. The reconciliation duet section 5 in B-flat, as stated, brings a clear *Ursatz* based on $\hat{3}$ (*d²*). The two following sections in G go together not only tonally, but structurally: the agitated section 6 reaches preliminary closure on $\hat{1}$ at the Countess' entry, but as a whole it makes a large-scale half-cadence (or 'interruption') onto $\hat{2}$/V, while the forgiveness scene (section 7), as stated earlier, recaptures $\hat{5}$(*d²*) as the basis for an *Ursatz* in G.

The next system presents a global interpretation of these structures. The initial headnote *f#²* is shown as being prolonged all the way from the initial section to the final one, by means of a large-scale neighbor *g²*, with the $\hat{3}$-$\hat{2}$-$\hat{1}$ descent in section 1 interpreted as a middleground event. (This structural predominance of the melody-note *g²* throughout sections 2–7 correlates with the critical function of the key of G major, discussed above, as the mediating key between the tonic D and the remote E-flat and B-flat.) Admittedly, in these middle sections *g²* actually functions as the headnote only in no. 4 in E-flat, but there it does so massively. (This the reason that the manipulation of register mentioned above doesn't affect the overall reading: *g²* governs the melody in any case.) In the G-major sections *d²* is the headnote; *g²* does not even enter on this layer until after the first section in this key (no. 2) is over.[38] (The *b* and *b♭* to which sections 2 and 5 descend are interpreted as descents into an inner part, while the remote keys E-flat and B-flat function as ♭VI and ♭III of G.) Where *g²* comes into its own is at the end of section 7 and the transition to the concluding *stretta* (Example 7). It was noted above that *g²* is prominent in section 7, and that the pitch-class *g*, indeed the pitch *g²*, is maintained unbroken through the orchestral transition, through to the beginning of section 8 on the unusual run-on V^7 chord. All this creates an indissoluble link between these two sections, not merely on the basis of the through-composed IV–V^7–I progression, but by the suspension of the deep-middleground *g²* from a consonant member of IV

38. See the diagonal line; such 'displacement' of an important melody note to a later position than its supporting bass is a common phenomenon.

into the dissonant 7th of the V^7 chord, which in turn must resolve to $f\#^2$. The latter progression duly occurs, to initiate the $\hat{3}$-$\hat{2}$-$\hat{1}$ of the first strong cadence in D, in mm. 461–64. This explicitly resolves the structural neighbor-note $\hat{4}$ back to $\hat{3}$, from which the *Ursatz* now takes its appointed course. This relationship is shown in the bottom system in Example 8, a reduction of the preceding one, with an additional detail: the $c\#^2$ of the dominant seventh that initiates the *stretta* arises by a continuation of the middle-ground descent $\hat{3}$-$\hat{2}$-$\hat{1}$ from section 1.

* * *

In conclusion, let me return to the dramatic significance of this finale. The reading offered here, whatever its limitations (every reading has limitations), is more inclusive than most others in current discourse — for example, those by Joseph Kerman and Allanbrook. Kerman, in keeping with his famous (or notorious) view that in opera the (only) dramatist is the composer, interprets the reconciliation scene between the Count and the Countess as a touchstone of Mozart's 'transcendence':

> Most important ... is Mozart's transformation of the ending of the play. With Beaumarchais, the reconciliation is nothing — worse than nothing, it suggests fatally that the intricate plot had beaten the author, and that clemency was the only way he saw to unravel it. As for Da Ponte, here is his contribution:

Ct	Contessa perdono.	Countess, forgive me.
Cts	Più docile io sono	I am more compliant,
	E dico di sì.	And say Yes.
Tutti	Ah tutti contenti	Ah, happy we all
	Saremo così.	Thus will be.

> With this miserable material before him, Mozart built a revelation.... In opera, the dramatist is the composer.[39]

But there is nothing 'miserable' about Da Ponte's verses here; they were more than adequate to support a musical resolution — as Mozart's treatment of them proves.

39. *Opera as Drama*, p. 91 (translation modified).

Kerman's dismissal of Da Ponte's text is symptomatic of a larger and more serious blind spot. In his eagerness to see the Count and Countess as real people with real feelings — as the main characters, those whose reconciliation is the hinge of the entire drama — he is shockingly, indeed bewilderingly, unsympathetic to Figaro and Susanna:

> Their feelings are more or less trivial.... Their reconciliation is correspondingly superficial, for they are safely behind their *commedia dell'arte* masks when all is forgiven....
>
> Mozart clearly intended nobility of station to symbolize nobility of spirit.... The Count and Countess are conscious; they feel their feelings through, and there is a ground of sympathy between them which Figaro and Susanna cannot ever comprehend.... The Count will soon be philandering again. But just as surely there will be another reconciliation, another renewal as genuine on both sides, as contrite and as beautiful. Clever Figaro and Susanna are not actually so secure.[40]

This seems to me a fundamental misreading, both of Figaro and Susanna as they are portrayed in the drama and by Mozart's music, and of the genre of which *Le nozze di Figaro* is a supreme representative. (It is their wedding-day, after all, that the opera celebrates; from another perspective, it is their roles that were created by the *primo buffo* and *prima donna* of the company, Francesco Benucci and Nancy Storace.) The assumption that '*commedia dell'arte* masks' are to be interpreted as a retreat into superficiality betrays a 19th- and 20th-century, 'realistic' view of drama, which in the context of 18th-century opera is anachronistic and largely irrelevant.

Allanbrook, by contrast, has no lack of sympathy for Figaro and Susanna, and understands perfectly that *commedia dell'arte* is potentially compatible with the highest drama,[41] which in the case of *Figaro* she interprets as a variety of pastoral (another unfairly maligned genre). However, analogously to Kerman but

40. Ibid. pp. 89–90.
41. 'Mozart's Happy Endings'.

oppositely, she overemphasizes the reconciliation between 'her' couple, Figaro and Susanna, and underestimates that between the Countess and Count, upon which she comments only in passing (pp. 192–93). I suspect a correlation between this underestimation and Allanbrook's univalent reading of the finale as an A–B–A form, in terms of the categories 'public' and 'private' (cf. above). For example, although correctly noting the diatonic-remote-diatonic tonal construction, she comments that both diatonic portions in their entirety represent 'the mechanical winding-down of the comedy', and interprets the reconciliation between Countess and Count as mere 'ceremony' (p. 186).

I find far more persuasive an interpretation of *Figaro* in terms of multiple and co-equal plots (as outlined above), which together create and reinforce its theme of the realization of human affection in society (however temporary we may believe the Count's conversion to be). In the finale, the structural role of g^2 in all the sections but the first and last strongly correlates with both the surface form and the dramatic course: the central sections in which the two primary subplots are played out and resolved are governed by non-tonic keys and by a non-triad pitch in the melody. In addition, the Schenkerian analysis is more nearly adequate to the dramatic action than the formal template of an A–B–A or an 'arch'; the drive towards dramatic resolution is accompanied, if not indeed 'motivated', by the dynamic, dissonant status of that g^2. Even the final, most affecting reconciliation, for all its foreground beauty and stability, takes place in a tonal space that cannot bring structural closure. Only the communal *lieto fine* can accomplish that.

PERSONALIA

JULIAN RUSHTON

Julian Rushton studied at Cambridge and for his doctorate at Oxford, supervised by J.A. Westrup. He taught at the University of East Anglia and subsequently at Cambridge, holding a fellowship at King's College (1974-81), before being appointed to the West Riding Chair of Music at the University of Leeds. He retired in 2005 and now lives in the Pennines near Huddersfield. Alongside numerous publications, he contributed the Mozart entries for *The New Grove Dictionary of Opera* and he is the author of *Mozart* in the Master Musicians Series, and of the Cambridge Music Handbook on *Don Giovanni*. He served as President of the Royal Musical Association (1994-9), and is chairman of the Editorial Committee of *Musica Britannica* (since 1993). He was appointed corresponding member of the American Musicological Society in 2000, and serves on the Directorium of the International Musicological Society (2007).

SERGIO DURANTE

Sergio Durante studied Music and Musicology at the University and at the Conservatory in Bologna. After a few years spent working as a practical musician, he turned his interests to Historical Musicology entering the Graduate School of Arts and Sciences at Harvard University in 1985 and completing a Ph.D program in 1993. His main musicological focus is methodology, investigated through studies on specific subjects ranging from Italian seventeenth century to the Classical period (Mozart in particular), to electro-acoustic music of the twentieth century. He has published essays in Italy, Germany, Austria, England, France, and Spain devoting his energies in recent years to Mozart studies in particular (becoming a member of the Mozart Academy in Salzburg in 2000).

STEFAN ROHRINGER

Stefan Rohringer studied music education, piano, music theory, musicology and history in Cologne. He is Professor of Music Theory at the University of Music and Performing Arts Munich (Hochschule für Musik und Theater München) and has published on a wide range of music pedagogical and theoretical topics. From 2004–2008 he served as President of the Gesellschaft für Musiktheorie (GMTH). Since 2006 he has been Co-Editor of the *Zeitschrift der Gesellschaft für Musiktheorie* (ZGMTH).

JAMES WEBSTER

James Webster is the Goldwin Smith Professor of Music at Cornell University. He specializes in the history and theory of music of the eighteenth and nineteenth centuries, with a particular focus on Haydn. His other interests include Mozart (especially his operas), Beethoven, Schubert, and Brahms, as well as performance practice, editorial practice, and the historiography of music; in theory he specializes in issues of musical form (including analytical methodology) and Schenkerian analysis. He has received the Einstein and Kinkeldey Awards of the American Musicological Society, a Fulbright dissertation grant, two Senior Research Fellowships from the National Endowment for the Humanities, a Guggenheim Fellowship, and a Research Fellowship of the Alexander von Humboldt Foundation (Germany). Webster served as President of the American Musicological Society. He is a Fellow of the American Academy of Arts and Sciences, a member of the Executive Committee of the Board of Directors of the Joseph Haydn Institute, and a member of the editorial board of *18th-Century Music*.

DARLA CRISPIN – EDITOR

Darla Crispin is a Fellow in Artistic Research at the Orpheus Research Centre in Music (ORCiM), Ghent, Flanders. A Canadian pianist and scholar, Dr. Crispin has worked as a solo performer and accompanist in the UK, Continental Europe and Canada, specializing in musical modernity in both her performing and her scholarship. Her work in the conservatoire sector has involved leadership of postgraduate studies at the Guildhall School of Music and Drama, followed by five-year tenure as Head of Graduate School at the Royal College of Music, which she carried out until 2008. Dr. Crispin's most recent scholarly work focuses upon the ramifications of practice-based research for musicians, scholars and audiences. Publications on this theme include 'Schoenberg's Wounded Work: Interpretative Themes and the *String Quartet in F sharp minor Opus 10,* in *Austrian Studies 17*' (Manley Publishing, for the Modern Humanities Research Association), and a collaborative volume with Kathleen Coessens and Anne Douglas, *The Artistic Turn: A Manifesto* (Orpheus Institute, September 2009). She is currently working on a book entitled *The Second Viennese School: Performance and Ethics and Understanding.*

FINAL EDITING
Darla Crispin

COPY EDITING
Kathleen Snyers

AUTHORS
Julian Rushton
Stefan Rohringer
Sergio Durante
James Webster

LAY-OUT
Jurgen Leemans
designed by Filiep Tacq

ISBN 978 90 5867 845 4
D/2012/1869/18
NUR 663

GPRC
Guaranteed
Peer Reviewed
Content
boekenvak.be/gprc

#1 INTER DISCIPLINAS ARS

Michel Butor, Henri Pousseur, Herman Sabbe, Silvio Senn

Inter Disciplinas Ars contains four reflections on music from a multidisciplinary approach: literature, Music pedagogy, Music sociology and philosophy

ISBN 9061869293 – 1998
Also available in Dutch: Inter Disciplinas Ars (ISBN 906186917x)

#2 THEORY INTO PRACTICE

Composition, Performance and Listening Experience
Nicholas Cook, Peter Johnson, Hans Zender

The central theme of this book is the relationship between the reflections about and the realization of a musical composition.

ISBN 9061869943 – 1999
Also available in Dutch: Theorie in Praktijk.Compositie, uitvoering en luister-ervaring (ISBN 9061869935)

#3 CAHIER «M»

A brief Morphology of Electric Sound.
Dick Raaijmakers

CAHIER-M is about the morphology of electric sound. Particular attention is given to the morphological relationship between the typically uniform nature of electric sound and the multi-layered sound structures used by post-WWII serial composers.

ISBN 9058670759 – 2005 (REPRINT)
Also available in Dutch: Cahier « M ». Kleine Morfologie van de elektrische klank. (ISBN 9058670767)

#4 ORDER AND DISORDER

Music-Theoretical Strategies in 20th-Century Music
Jonathan Dunsby, Joseph N. Strauss, Yves Knockaert, Max Paddison, Konrad Boehmer

Order and Disorder discusses theoretical, historical and philosophical aspects of music and theory after the 1950s in relation to performance practice.

ISBN 9058673693 – 2004

#5 IDENTITY AND DIFFERENCE

Essays on Music, Language and Time
Jonathan Cross, Jonathan Harvey, Helmut Lachenmann, Albrecht Wellmer, Richard Klein

Identity and Difference collects five writings on the relationship between music and language and music and time, from the view of composers, musicologists, critics, philosophers and music theorists.

ISBN 9058674134 – 2004

#6 TOWARDS TONALITY

Aspects of Baroque Music Theory
Thomas Christensen, Penelope Gouk, Gérard Geay, Susan McClary, Markus Jans, Joel Lester, Marc Vanscheeuwijck

Towards Tonality considers the often complex connections and intersections between modal and tonal idioms, contrapuntal and harmonic organisation, from various perspectives as to the transition (towards tonality) from the Renaissance to the Baroque era.

ISBN 9789058675873 – 2007

#7 NEW PATHS

Aspects of Music Theory and Aesthetics in the Age of Romanticism

John Neubauer, Janet Schmalfeldt, Scott Burnham, Susan Youens, Jim Samson

New Paths focuses on a broad range of issues on nineteenth century music in a re-contextualising and fresh manner: the concept of organicism, the musical evolution of Beethovens 'Bridgetower' Sonata, the staging of subjectivity in Beethoven's late music, Franz Lachner and the limits of the Lied and the environmental influences on Chopin's work.

ISBN 9789058677341 – 2009

#8 UNFOLDING TIME

Studies in Temporality in Twentieth Century Music

Bruce Brubaker, Pascal Decroupet, Mark Delaere, Justin London, Ian Pace

For performers, the primary perception of music is arguably the way in which it unfolds in 'real time'; while for composers a work appears 'whole and entire', with the presence of the score having the potential to compress, and even eliminate, the perception of time as 'passing'. The paradoxical relationship between these two perspectives, and the subtle mediations at the interface between them, form the subject matter of this collection of studies.

ISBN 9789058677358 – 2009

#9 PARTIMENTO AND CONTINUO PLAYING

In Theory and in Practice

Thomas Christensen, Robert Gjerdingen, Giorgio Sanguinetti, Rudolf Lutz

The point of departure for *Partimento* was not 'Music Theory' as such, but the interaction between music theory, music history, performance practice, aesthetics, and related sciences. Thomas Christensen, shows how the development of tonal harmonic theory went hand in hand with the practice of thoroughbass. Both Robert Gjerdingen and Giorgio Sanguinetti focus on the Neapolitan tradition of partimento. Gjerdingen addresses the relation between the realization of partimenti and contrapuntal thinking, illustrated by examples of contrapuntal imitation and combination in partimenti, leading to the 'partimentofugue'. Sanguinetti elaborates on the history of this partimentofugue from the early 18th until the late 19th century. Finally, Rudolf Lutz presents his use of partimenti in educational practice, giving examples of how reviving this old practice can give new insights to composers, conductors and musicians.

ISBN 978 90 5867 828 7 – 2010

---

01. The Artistic Turn: a manifesto
Kathleen Coessens, Darla Crispin, Anne Douglas

Charts a constellation of ideas for a new paradigm — a 'turn' — that outlines the burgeoning discipline of artistic research and points to its manifold and open-ended possibilities through its re-emphasis of the centrality of the artist.

ISBN 9789490389000 – 2009

---

02. metaCage: Essays on and around Freeman Etudes, Fontana Mix, Aria
Magnus Andersson, William Brooks, Mieko Kanno, Juan Parra Cancino

Investigates the musical practice of John Cage in four essays written by ORCiM Fellows. Three works (Fontana Mix, Aria, and Freeman Etudes) serve as threads that link the contributions. The essays embrace both compositional practice, as viewed by musicologically-oriented performers Juan Parra Cancino and Mieko Kanno, and Cage's aesthetic framework, explored by practice-based musicologists Magnus Andersson and William Brooks.

ISBN 9789490389017 – 2009

---

03. **Dynamics of Constraints**
Essays on Notation, Editing and Performance
Mieko Kanno, Paulo de Assis, Juan Parra Cancino

Expresses some fundamental issues addressed by ORCiM's research group 'the musician's relation to notation'. Paulo de Assis argues that critical editions should generate critical users, advocating a new kind of editor and performer; Mieko Kanno's contribution reflects the rapid expansion of the use of electronics in contemporary music, while Juan Parra Cancino points towards a kind of composition, where both the performing and the listening experience do not aim to achieve a 'final' version of the piece.

ISBN 9789490389024 – 2009

04. **The Practice of Practising**

Alessandro Cervino, Catherine Laws, Maria Lettberg, Tânia Lisboa

The process of practising is intrinsic to musical creativity. Practising may primarily be thought of as technical, but it is often also musically meaningful, including elements of interpretation, improvisation, and/or composition. The practice room can be a space in which to explore a field of creative possibilities; a place to experiment and to refine ideas. To date, the literature on practice has been primarily pedagogical and psychological. Little attention is paid to the significance of practice, and especially to the role of embodied experience — of understanding gained through doing — in the forming of musical ideas. *The Practice of Practising* is primarily concerned with considering practising as a practice in itself: a collection of processes that determines musical creativity and significance. The volume comprises four diverse case studies, in relation to music by J. S. Bach, Elliott Carter, Alfred Schnittke, and Morton Feldman, presenting both solo and ensemble perspectives.

ISBN 978 90 5867 848 5 - 2011

Both series are available at Leuven University Press: **www.upers.kuleuven.be**